THE ART OF TRANSCRIBING

DRUM SET • BOOK 1

BY ALAN SCHECHNER

Online Audio www.melbay.com/20814BCDEB

Audio Contents

1	Quarter Notes	18	Rhythm #7 Ex. (1-6)	36	Random Sixteenth Combo Ex. (1-6) *cont.*	50	Rhythm #4 Ex. (1-6)
2	Eighth Notes	19	Rhythm #8 (prep)	37	Random Hi-hat Combo	51	Rhythm #5 (prep)
3	Sixteenth Notes	20	Rhythm #8 Ex. (1-6)	38	Random Hi-hat Combo Ex. (1-6)	52	Rhythm #5 Ex. (1-6)
4	Straight Feel: Hi-Hat Rhythm	21	Rhythm #9 (prep)	39	Random Combo (everything) Ex. (1-6)	53	Rhythm #6 (prep)
5	Rhythm #1 (prep)	22	Rhythm #9 Ex. (1-6)	40	Random Fills Ex. (1-9)	54	Rhythm #6 Ex. (1-6)
6	Rhythm #1 Ex. (1-6)	23	Rhythm #10 (prep)	41	Eighth Note Triplets	55	Rhythm #7 (prep)
7	Rhythm #2 (prep)	24	Rhythm #10 Ex. (1-6)	42	Triplet Feel: Hi-Hat Rhythm	56	Rhythm #7 Ex. (1-6)
8	Rhythm #2 Ex. (1-6)	25	Rhythm #11 (prep)	43	Rhythm #1 (prep)	57	Random Triplet Combo Ex. (1-6)
9	Rhythm #3 (prep)	26	Rhythm #11 Ex. (1-6)	44	Rhythm #1 Ex. (1-6)	58	Random Hi-hat Combo
10	Rhythm #3 Ex. (1-6)	27	Rhythm #12 (prep)	45	Rhythm #2 (prep)	59	Random Hi-hat Combo Ex. (1-6)
11	Rhythm #4 (prep)	28	Rhythm #12 Ex. (1-6)	46	Rhythm #2 Ex. (1-6)	60	Random Combo (everything) Ex. (1-6)
12	Rhythm #4 Ex. (1-6)	29	Rhythm #13 (prep)	47	Rhythm #3 (prep)	61	Random Triplet Fills Ex. (1-9)
13	Rhythm #5 (prep)	30	Rhythm #13 Ex. (1-6)	48	Rhythm #3 Ex. (1-6)		
14	Rhythm #5 Ex. (1-6)	31	Rhythm #14 (prep)	49	Rhythm #4 (prep)		
15	Rhythm #6 (prep)	32	Rhythm #14 Ex. (1-6)				
16	Rhythm #6 Ex. (1-6)	33	Rhythm #15 (prep)				
17	Rhythm #7 (prep)	34	Rhythm #15 Ex. (1-6)				
		35	Random Sixteenth Combo Ex. (1-6)				

3 4 5 6 7 8 9 0

Visit us on the Web at www.melbay.com — E-mail us at email@melbay.com

Table of Contents

Notation Key

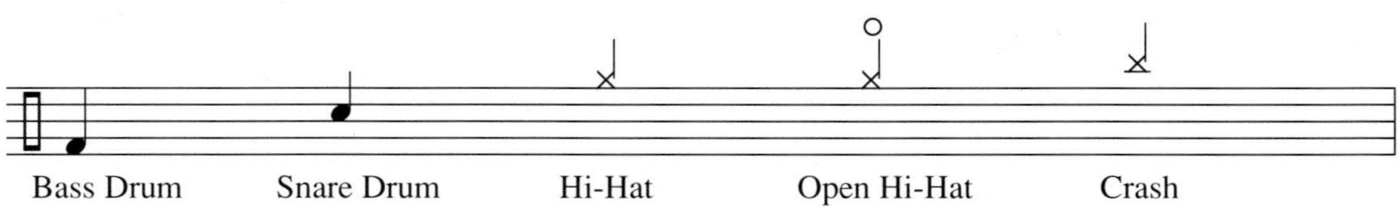

Special thanks to:
Jeffrey Winslow for your time, energy and generosity with the making of the audio! Rob Leytham for your relentless encouragement and friendship! My wife Rose, my parents Barbara and Jules and my brother Steve, Chuck Brown, Jeremy Colson, everybody at The Magic Flute, Robert Bowler at A Drummer's Tradition, Tony Williams and Patrick McCormick at Music Star Productions, Mr. William Bay, Sheri Schleusner, Julie Price, Shawnna Troxel, and the incredible staff at Mel Bay Publications.

How to Use the Book & Audio

1) Learn a rhythm - The even numbered pages in Section One and Two will introduce one new rhythm at a time. I recommend that you play along with the audio. In addition, make sure to look at the rhythm as you play.This will help you to associate the sound of the rhythm with the written notation.

2) Transcribe the beats/fills - The odd numbered pages in Section One and Two will apply each new rhythm to the drum set (bass, snare and hi-hat). Listen to the audio and transcribe the beats/fills on to the blank music paper that is provided.

3)*Check your accuracy - When you finish transcribing each page, simply turn to pages 62-82 for the answers.

*Proofreading

Before you peek at the answers, make sure that you play your transcription. You will know that you are correct if the beat that you play sounds like the beat from the audio. If it sounds different, you will probably be able to determine any changes that you will need to make. I like to think of this as musical proofreading. This is the same process that you would use when you write a sentence. Most likely you would proofread to make sure that your spelling is correct.

ATTENTION TEACHERS: Try playing the beats on the drum set for your students (or program the beats into a drum machine). This will:
A) Allow you to slow down the tempo for beginning students.
B) Allow you to speed up the tempo for advanced students.
C) Allow you to continuously loop the patterns until the student has finished each transcription.

Note: Make sure that the student does not watch you play. It is important that they develop their listening skills.

What is Transcribing?

Transcribing simply means to write down. It could be anything from a beat, fill, solo or even a song.

Why Transcribe?

1) <u>To remember your ideas</u> - Have you ever created a groove or fill that you were really excited about and thought to yourself "I'll remember this?" What usually happens? You guessed it! We forget how we played it! If we were to have written it down (transcribed), it would not matter if we forgot how to play it because we would have a hard copy of the pattern to refer to.

2) <u>To learn songs quickly</u> - Suppose you had to learn 10 songs in a few days. If we rely simply on our memory, we might not have trouble learning the 1st or 2nd song. However, by the 3rd song it can become difficult to remember how the 1st song goes. Sound familiar? When we transcribe the basic grooves and fills of each song, we will have a quick reference chart that will guide us through new music. One bonus that I have discovered is I tend to memorize the music quicker simply by writing it down.

3) <u>To learn to play the ideas in our imagination</u> - When I want to learn to play a pattern that I am hearing in my head, I simply transcribe my idea. This will allow me to see and feel exactly how the hands and feet work together.This is a tremendous time saver. Also, I don't have to worry about forgetting my new idea because it's written down (See reason #1 above).

4) <u>To communicate our ideas</u> - Think about how many great drum books are available today. If the drummers who authored those books did not know how to transcribe their ideas, their books would not exist. Also, every time your drum teacher writes out a new rhythm for you to work on, he or she is using their transcribing skills. Just think, after you complete this book somebody might ask you, 'How did you play that amazing groove?' You will be able to communicate your idea through *The Art Of Transcribing.*

About the Musical Terms

There are many musical terms that will appear in this book which are essential for every musician to be familiar with. However, rather than listing a bunch of terms for you to memorize now, I have decided to highlight (in big bold letters) certain terms as *they naturally appear in the text.* This will allow you to learn as you go. For example, when you see a sentence such as :

It's time to start transcribing **beats** (see page 83).

Simply turn to page 83 for an explanation of the term 'beats'.

Note: The following terms will be defined visually - Stem, note head, flag, repeat sign, double bar, beam (page 6), double beam (page 7) and double flag (page 7).

Pre-section One

Before we start transcribing, let's learn three basic rhythms and the equivalent rests:

1) Quarter Notes
2) Eighth Notes
3) Sixteenth Notes

Understanding these rhythms will help tremendously in section one.

Quarter Notes

Turn on your metronome to any speed (I recommend starting slow). The metronome is playing quarter notes. Try hitting your snare drum on each click. Now you are playing quarter notes.

Here is the written notation for a quarter note: (Notice that a quarter note uses one note head and one stem)

Track 1

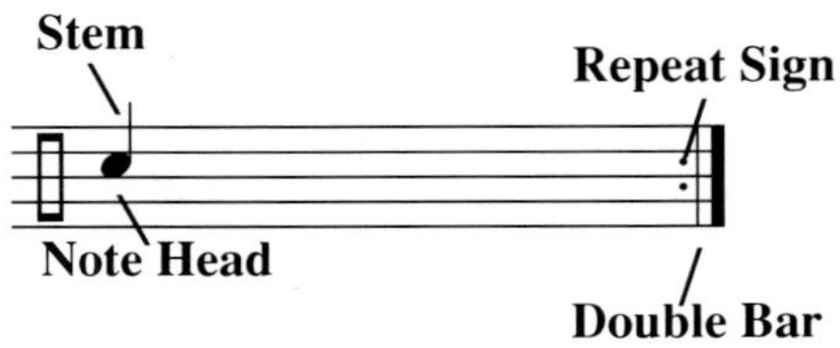

(The two dots next to the double bar tells us that the music is to be repeated).

Here is the written notation for a quarter note **rest** (see page 83):

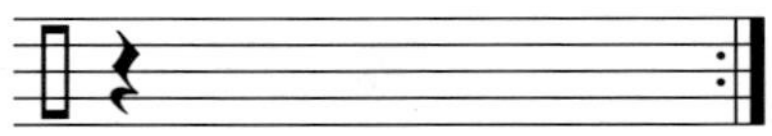

8th Notes

Next, play two evenly spaced hits (per click) along with your metronome. You are now playing 8th notes.

Here is the written notation for (two) 8th notes:

Track 2

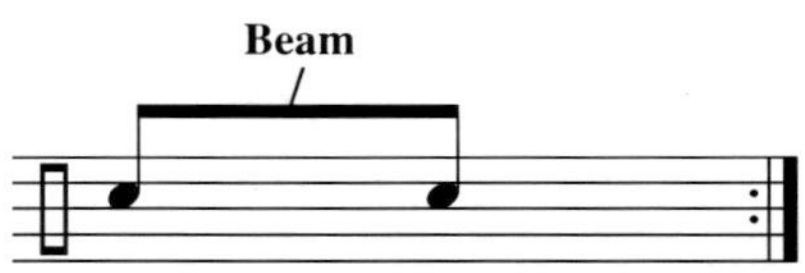

Here is the written notation for (two) 8th note rests:

Here is the written notation for one eighth note:

16th Notes

Finally, play four evenly spaced hits (per click) along with your metronome. You are now playing 16th notes.

Here is the written notation for 16th notes:

Track 3

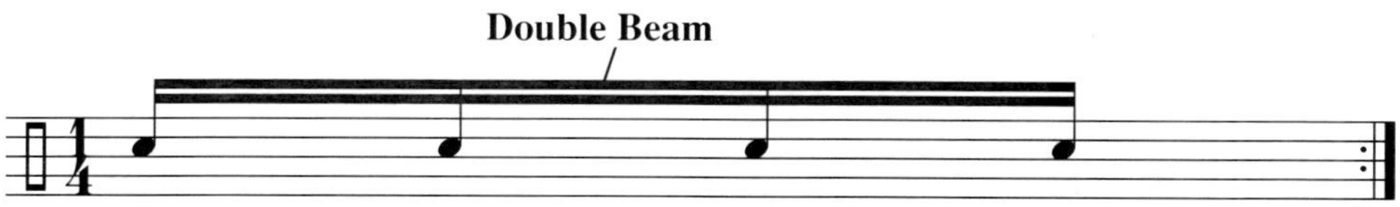

Here is the written notation for (four) 16th note rests:

Here is the written notation for one 16th note:

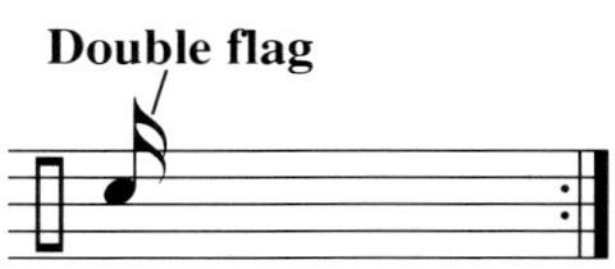

Section One

Straight Feel

It's time to start transcribing **beats** (see page 83 def. #1). *All* of the beats in section 1 (pages 9-37) will use the following eighth note hi-hat rhythm.

Track 4

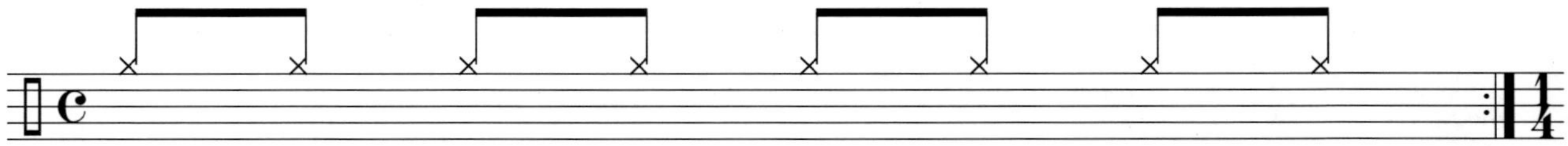

We will learn to incorporate <u>one rhythm at a time</u> *along with* the above hi-hat rhythm. The (fifteen) rhythms you are about to learn are **subdivisions** (see page 84) of sixteenth notes.

Rhythm #1 (prep.)

Rhythm #1 is *based upon* the <u>first 16th note</u> (of the four 16th notes per **beat** - see page 83 def. #2).This is illustrated below rhythm #1. See figure A.

Rhythm #1

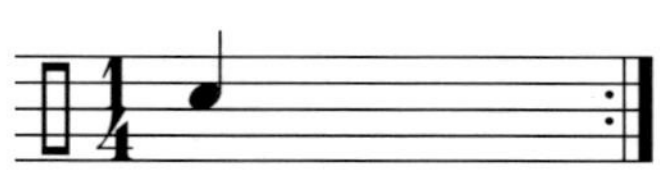

Figure A

Here is the prep. exercise for rhythm #1 written in **4/4** (see page 84). I recommend that you play along with the audio. Also, make sure to look at rhythm #1 as you play. This will help you to associate the sound of the rhythm with the written notation. Notice that this rhythm hits at the same time as the click (metronome).

Track 5

Remember, in this section all of the beats will use the following 8th note rhythm on the hi-hat. I recommend that you write out this cymbal rhythm on examples 2-6 now. Example #1 is provided for you.

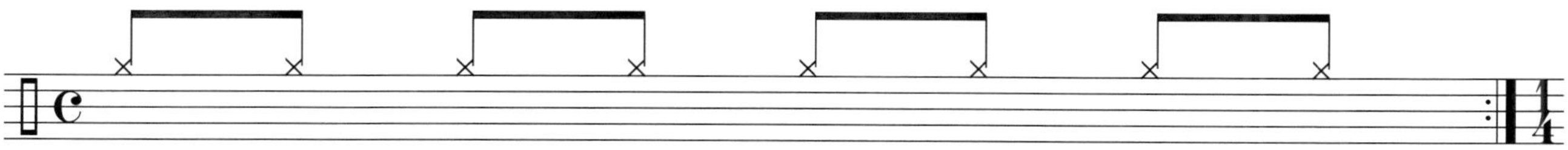

All of the beats on this page incorporate rhythm #1 (from page 8).

RHYTHM #1

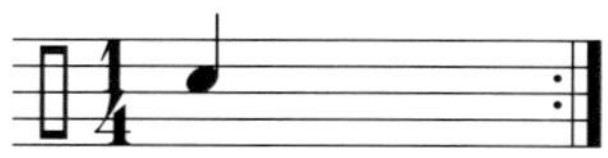

Here is rhythm #1 *combined* with the above cymbal pattern:

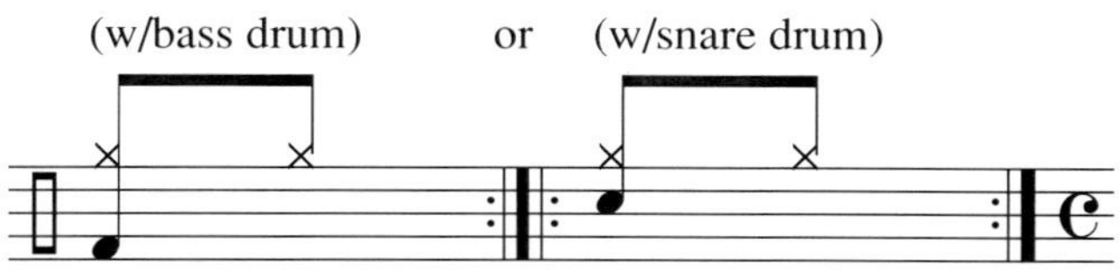

Track 6
EX. 1-6

*Listen to the audio and transcribe the following beats.

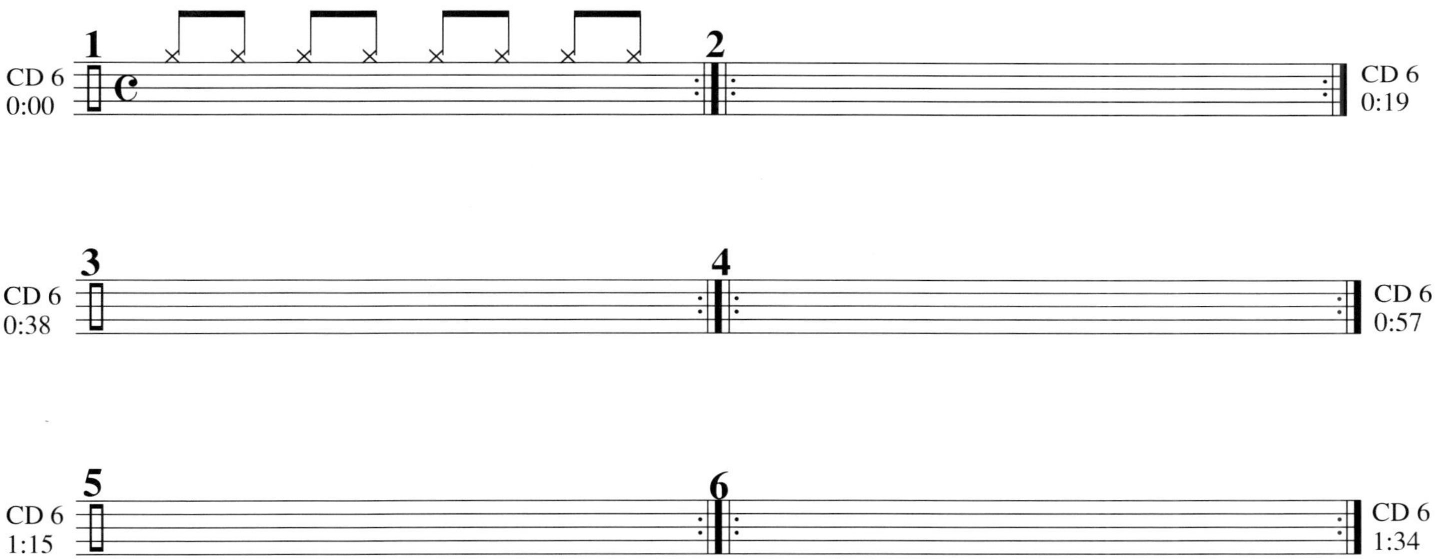

THE ANSWERS ARE ON PAGE 62

*You probably noticed that these beats use open hi-hat. This is notated simply by putting the letter 'O' above the appropriate note. For example, opening on the '&' of 4 would look like this:

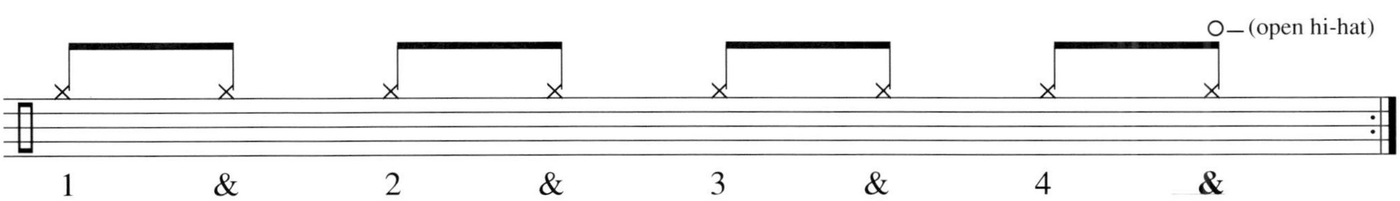

Rhythm #2 (prep.)

Rhythm #2 is *based upon* the <u>second 16th note</u> (of the four 16th notes per beat). This is illustrated below rhythm #2. See figure A.

Rhythm #2 

Figure A 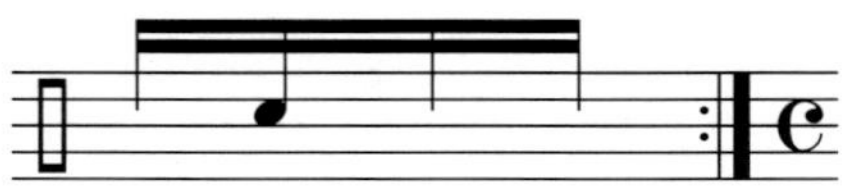

Here is the prep. exercise for rhythm #2 written in 4/4. I recommend that you *play along* with the audio. Make sure to look at rhythm #2 as you play. This will help you to associate the sound of the rhythm with the written notation. Also, notice that this rhyhm hits immediately after each click.

Track 7

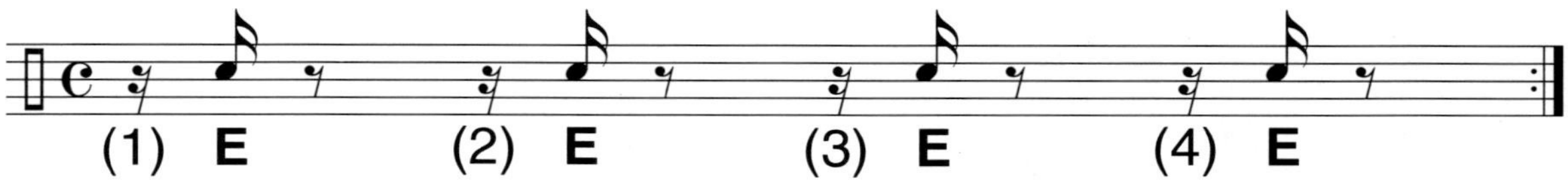

All of the beats on this page incorporate rhythm #2 (from page 10). *In addition, I will also include the bass drum on beats one and/or three as well as the snare drum on beats two and/or four.*

RHYTHM #2

Here is rhythm #2 *combined* with the 8th note cymbal pattern:

(w/bass drum) or (w/snare drum)

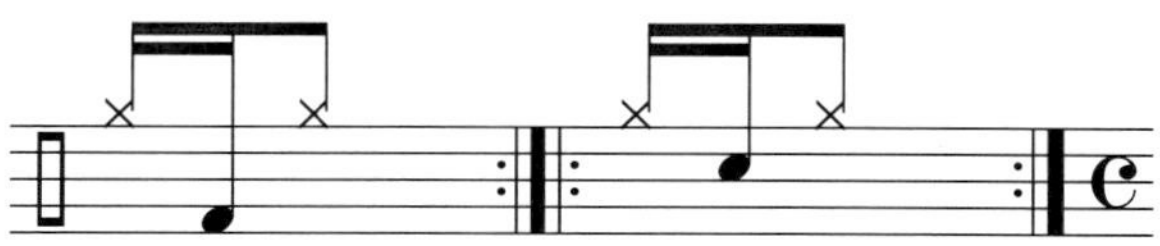

Listen to the audio and transcribe the following beats. Remember to start by writing the 8th note cymbal pattern. Once again, I have provided example 1 for you.

Track 8
EX. 1-6

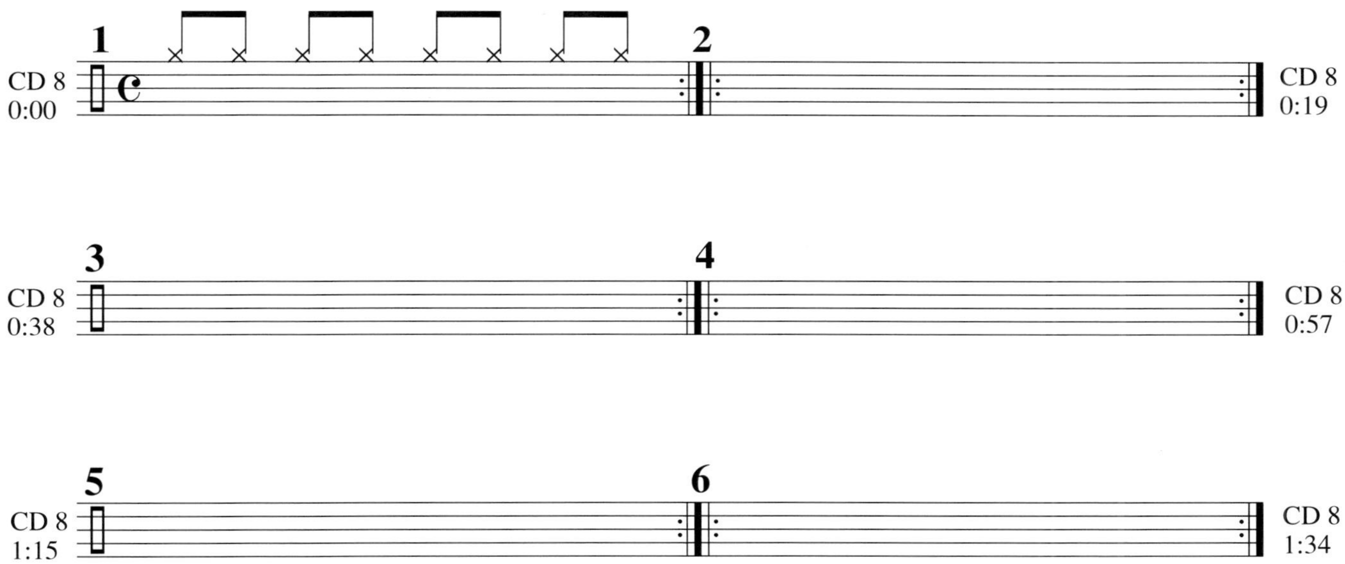

THE ANSWERS ARE ON PAGE 62

Rhythm #3 (prep.)

Rhythm #3 is *based upon* the <u>third 16th note</u> (of the four 16th notes per beat). This is illustrated below rhythm #3. See figure A.

Rhythm #3 

Figure A 

Here is the prep. exercise for rhythm #3 written in 4/4. I recommend that you *play along* with the audio. Make sure to look at rhythm #3 as you play. This will help you to associate the sound of the rhythm with the written notation. Also, notice the relationship between rhythm #3 and the click.

Track 9

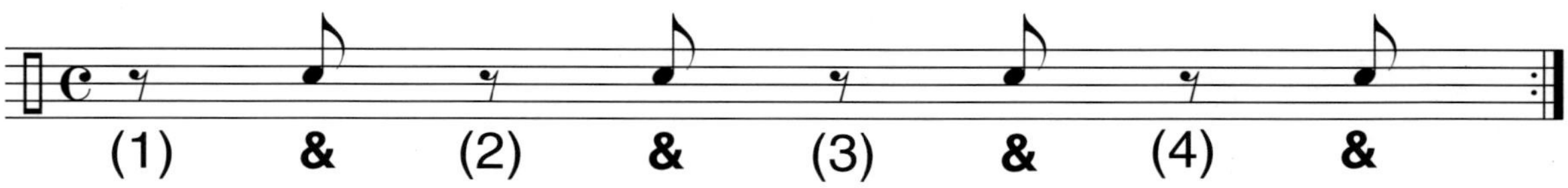

All of the beats on this page incorporate rhythm #3 (from page 12). *In addition, I will also include the bass drum on beats one and/or three as well as the snare drum on beats two and/or four.*

RHYTHM #3

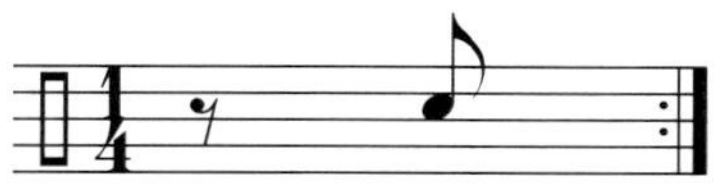

Here is rhythm #3 *combined* with the 8th note cymbal pattern:

(w/bass drum) or (w/snare drum)

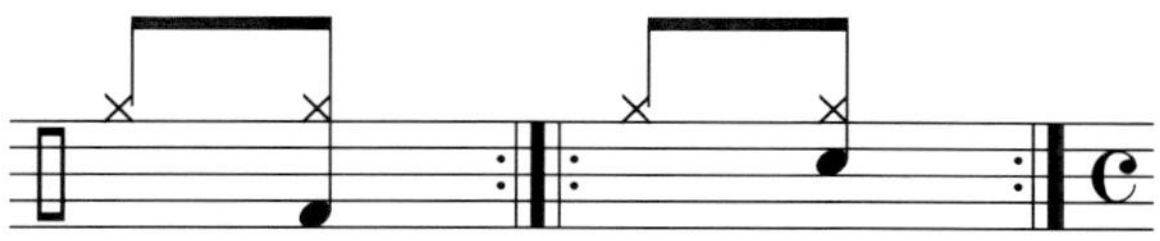

Listen to the audio and transcribe the following beats. Remember to start by writing the 8th note cymbal pattern.

Track 10
EX. 1-6

1 **2**

CD 10
0:00

CD 10
1:19

3 **4**

CD 10
0:37

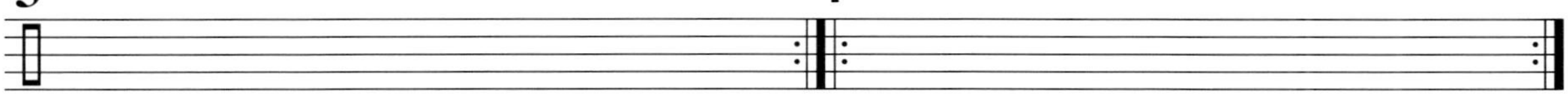

CD 10
0:56

5 **6**

CD 10
1:15

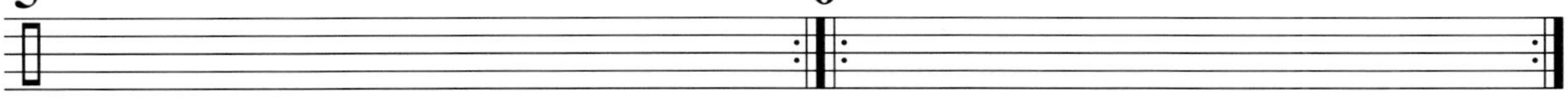

CD 10
1:34

THE ANSWERS ANSWERS ARE ON PAGE 63

Rhythm #4 (prep.)

Rhythm #4 is *based upon* the fourth 16th note (of the four 16th notes per beat). This is illustrated below rhythm #4. See figure A.

Rhythm #4*

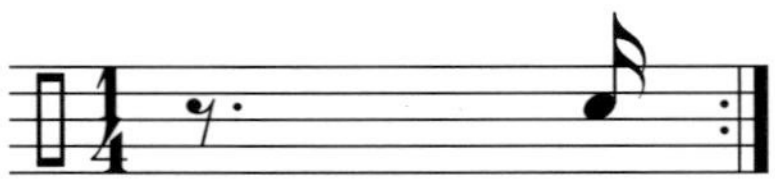

Figure A

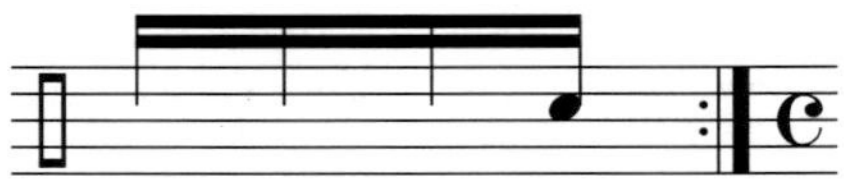

Here is the prep. exercise for rhythm #4 written in 4/4. I recommend that you *play along* with the audio. Make sure to look at rhythm #4 as you play. This will help you to associate the sound of the rhythm with the written notation. Also, notice the relationship between rhythm #4 and the click.

Track 11

*The dot next to the 8th note rest is equivalent to a 16th note rest.

All of the beats on this page incorporate rhythm #4 (from page 14). *In addition, I will also include the bass drum on beats one and/or three as well as the snare drum on beats two and/or four.*

RHYTHM #4

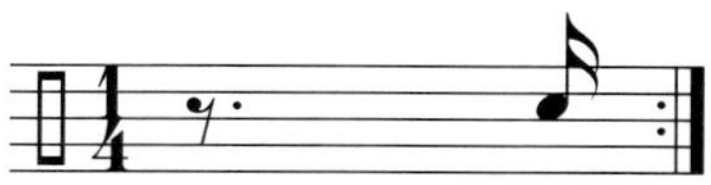

Here is rhythm #4 *combined* with the 8th note cymbal pattern:

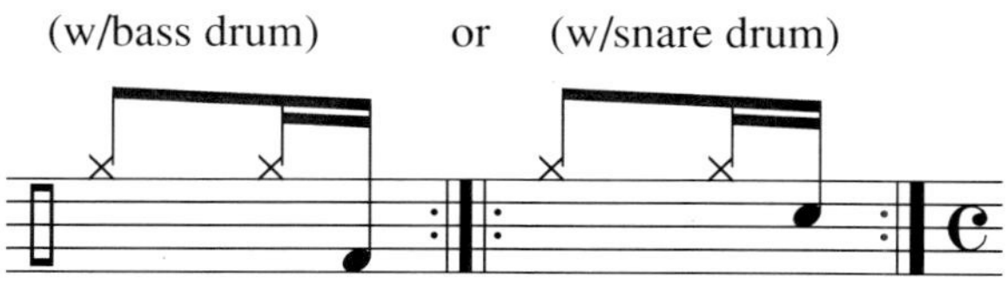

Listen to the audio and transcribe the following beats. Remember to start by writing the 8th note cymbal pattern.

Track 12
EX. 1-6

CD 12
0:00

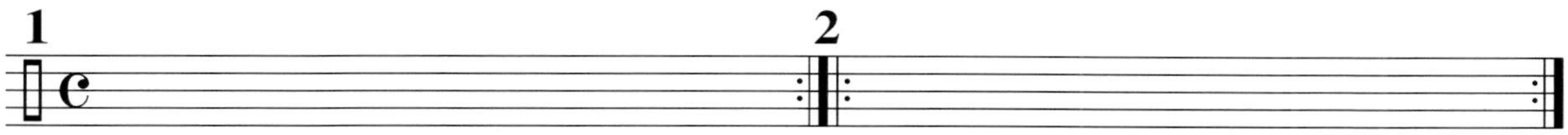

CD 12
0:19

CD12
0:37

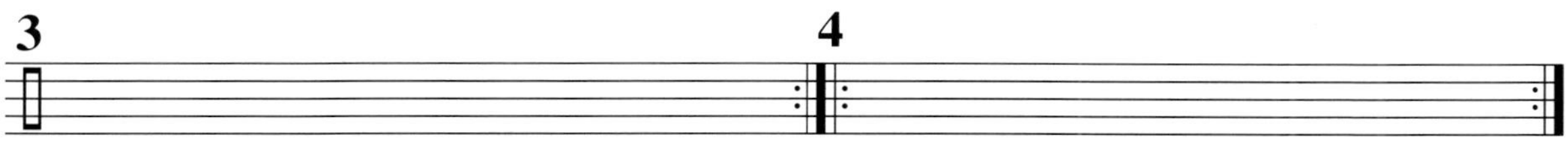

CD 12
0:55

CD 12
1:14

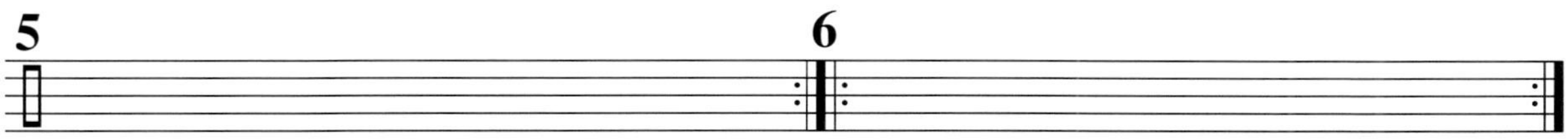

CD 12
1:33

THE ANSWERS ARE ON PAGE 63

Rhythm #5 (prep.)

Rhythm #5 is *based upon* the <u>first and second 16th note</u> (of the four 16th notes per beat). This is illustrated below rhythm #5. See figure A.

Rhythm #5 

Figure A 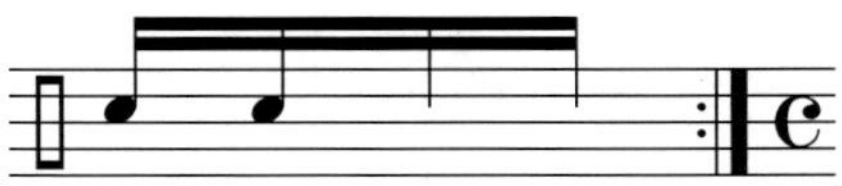

Here is the prep. exercise for rhythm #5 written in 4/4. I recommend that you *play along* with the audio. Make sure to look at rhythm #5 as you play. This will help you to associate the sound of the rhythm with the written notation. Also, notice the relationship between rhythm #5 and the click.

Track 13 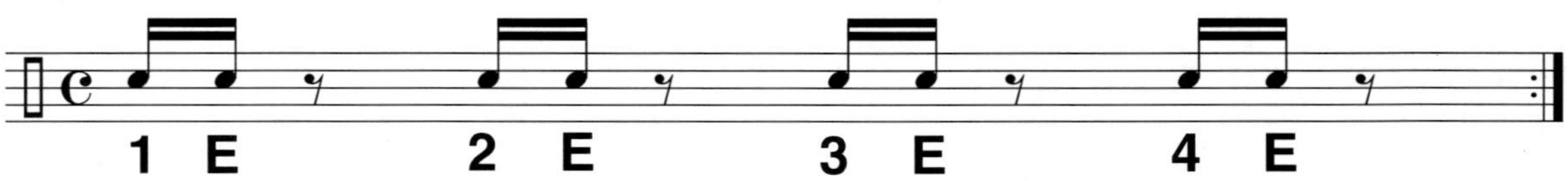

All of the beats on this page incorporate rhythm #5 (from page 16). *In addition, I will also include the bass drum on beats one and/or three as well as the snare drum on beats two and/or four.*

RHYTHM #5

Here is rhythm #5 *combined* with the 8th note cymbal pattern:

(w/bass drum) or (w/snare drum)

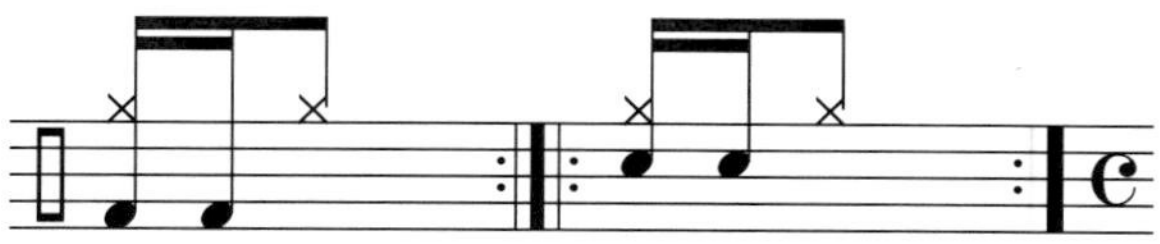

Listen to the audio and transcribe the following beats. Remember to start by writing the 8th note cymbal pattern.

Track 14
EX. 1-6

1 2

CD 14 0:00

CD 14 0:18

3 4

CD 14 0:37

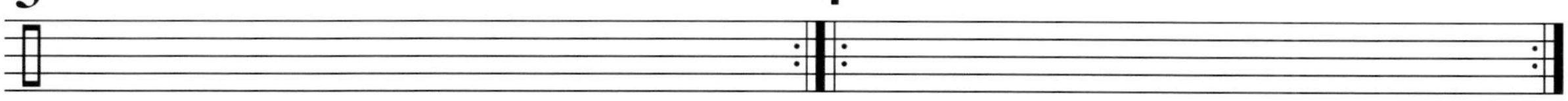

CD 14 0:55

5 6

CD 14 1:14

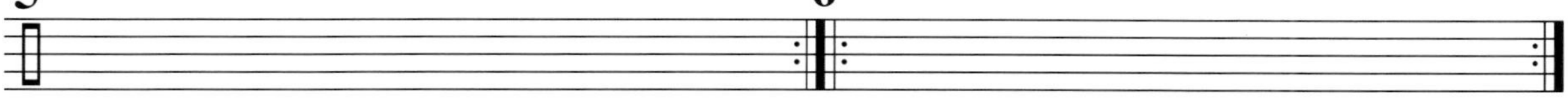

CD 14 1:33

THE ANSWERS ARE ON PAGE 64

Rhythm #6 (prep.)

Rhythm #6 is *based upon* the first and third 16th note (of the four 16th notes per beat). This is illustrated below rhythm #6. See figure A.

Rhythm #6 

Figure A 

Here is the prep. exercise for rhythm #6 written in 4/4. I recommend that you *play along* with the audio. Make sure to look at rhythm #6 as you play. This will help you to associate the sound of the rhythm with the written notation. Also, notice the relationship between rhythm #6 and the click.

Track 15

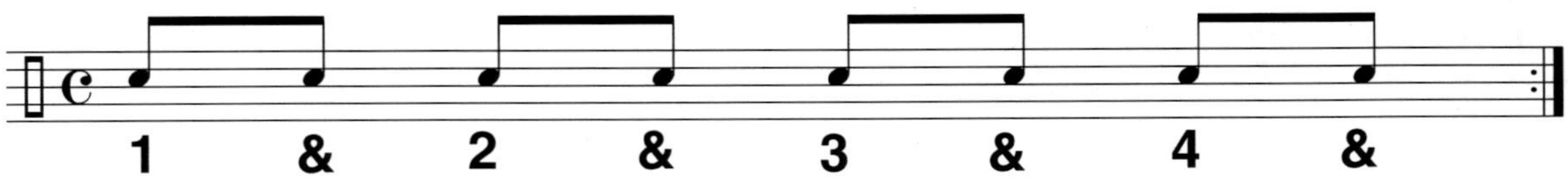

All of the beats on this page incorporate rhythm #6 (from page 18). *In addition, I will also include the bass drum on beats one and/or three as well as the snare drum on beats two and/or four.*

RHYTHM #6

Here is rhythm #6 *combined* with the 8th note cymbal pattern:

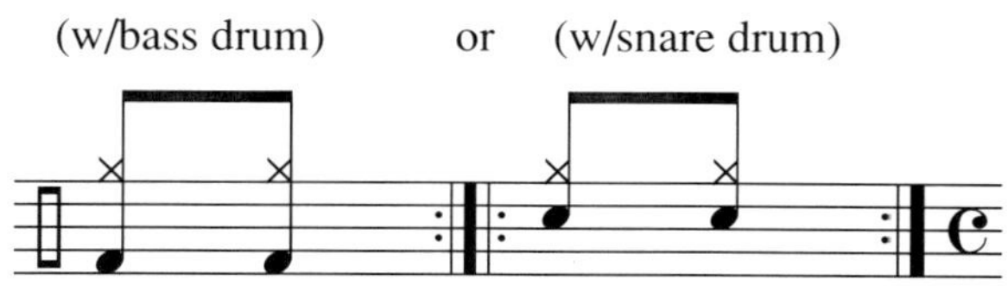

Listen to the audio and transcribe the following beats. Remember to start by writing the 8th note cymbal pattern.

Track 16
EX. 1-6

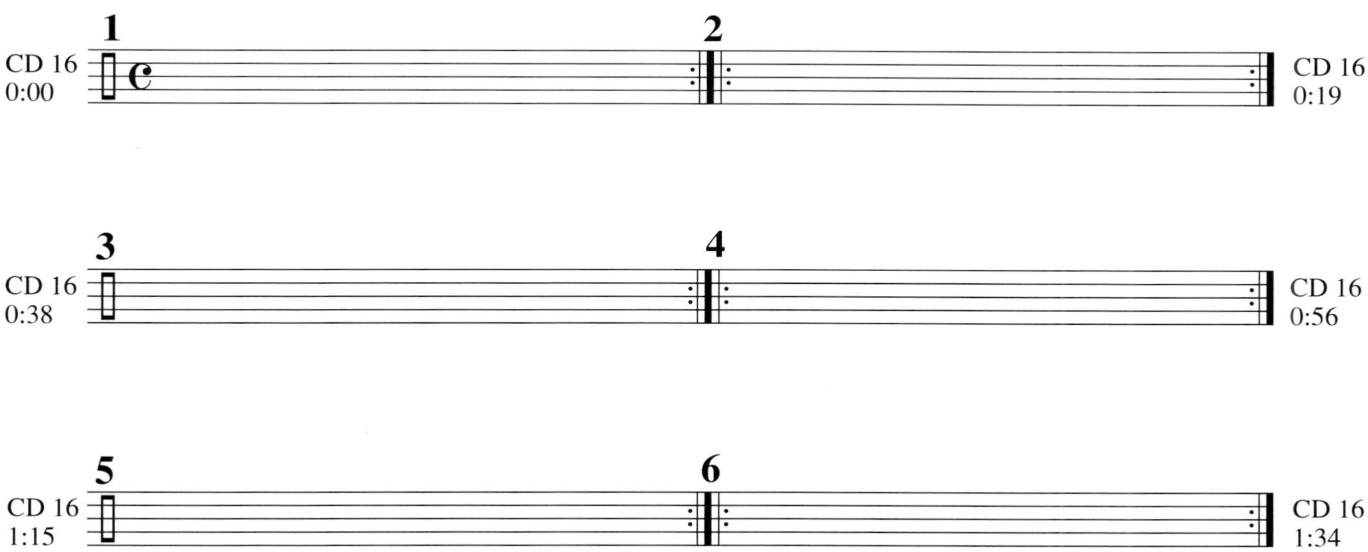

THE ANSWERS ARE ON PAGE 64

Rhythm #7 (prep.)

Rhythm #7 is *based upon* the first and fourth 16th note (of the four 16th notes per beat). This is illustrated below rhythm #7. See figure A.

* **Rhythm #7**

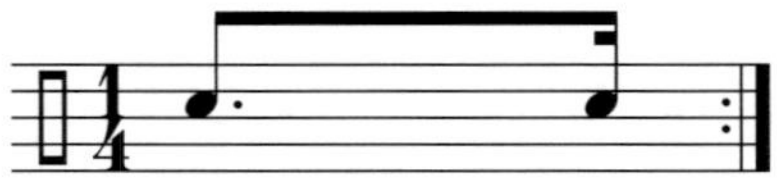

Figure A

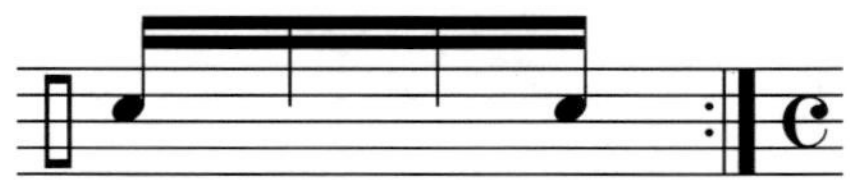

Here is the prep. exercise for rhythm #7 written in 4/4. I recommend that you *play along* with the audio. Make sure to look at rhythm #7 as you play. This will help you to associate the sound of the rhythm with the written notation. Also, notice the relationship between rhythm #7 and the click.

Track 17

*The dot next to the 8th note is equivalent to a 16th note rest.
(Technically, the dot is *increasing* the *duration* of the 8th note by a 16th note).

All of the beats on this page incorporate rhythm #7 (from page 20). *In addition, I will also include the bass drum on beats one and/or threeas well as the snare drum on beats two and/or four.*

RHYTHM #7

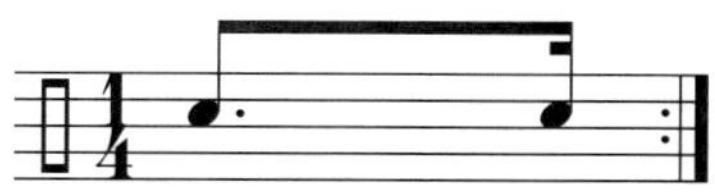

Here is rhythm #7 *combined* with the 8th note cymbal pattern:

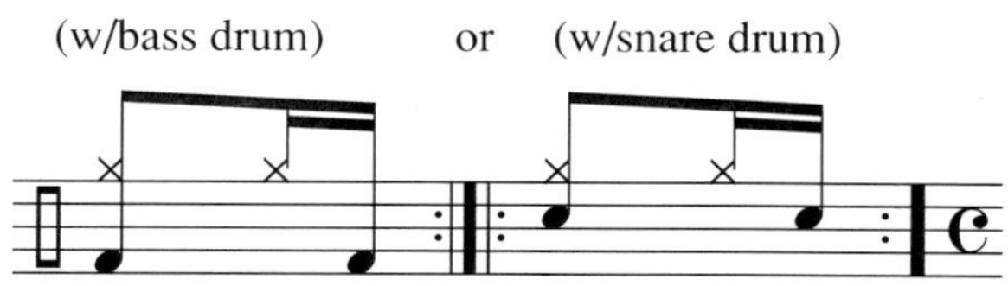

Listen to the audio and transcribe the following beats. Remember to start by writing the 8th note cymbal pattern.

Track 18
EX. 1-6

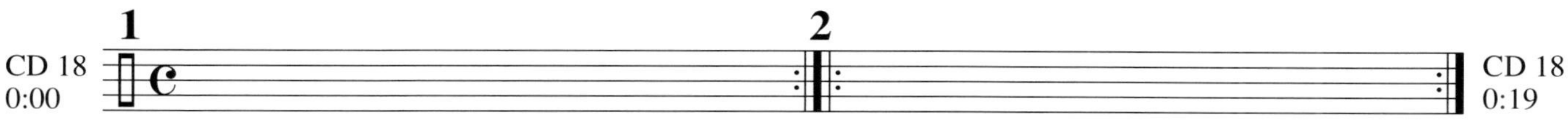

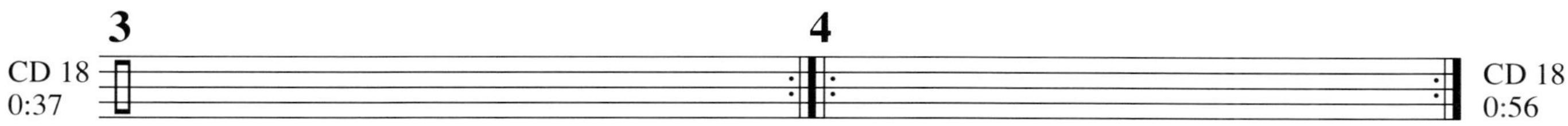

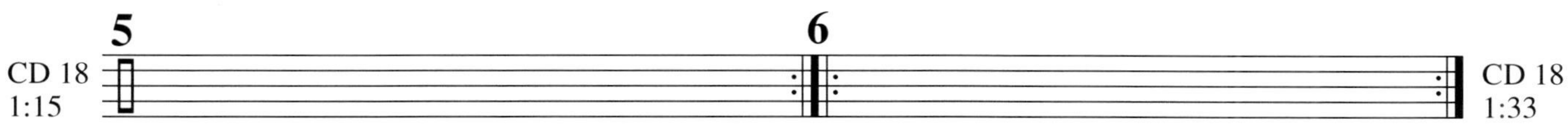

THE ANSWERS ARE ON PAGE 65

Rhythm #8 (prep.)

Rhythm #8 is *based upon* the <u>second and third 16th note</u> (of the four 16th notes per beat). This is illustrated below rhythm #8. See figure A.

Rhythm #8

Figure A

Here is the prep. exercise for rhythm #8 written in 4/4. I recommend that you *play along* with the audio. Make sure to look at rhythm #8 as you play. This will help you to associate the sound of the rhythm with the written notation. Also, notice the relationship between rhythm #8 and the click.

Track 19

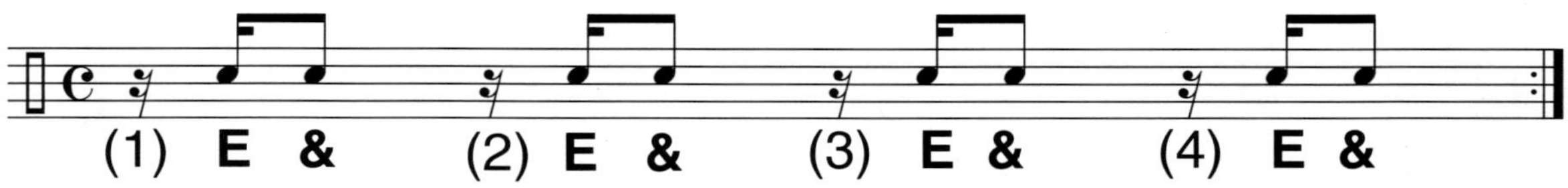

All of the beats on this page incorporate rhythm #8 (from page 22). In addition, I will also include the bass drum on beats one and/or three as well as the snare drum on beats two and/or four.

RHYTHM #8

Here is rhythm #8 *combined* with the 8th note cymbal pattern:

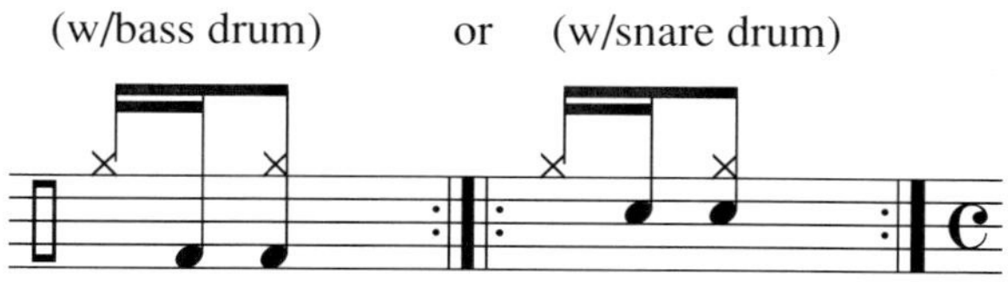

Listen to the audio and transcribe the following beats. Remember to start by writing the 8th note cymbal pattern.

Track 20
EX. 1-6

CD 20 0:00

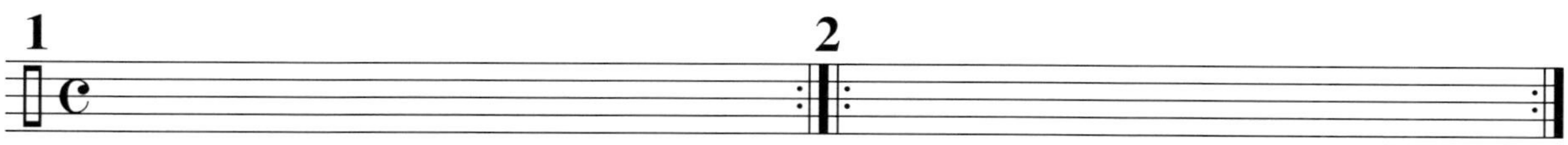

CD 20 0:19

CD 20 0:38

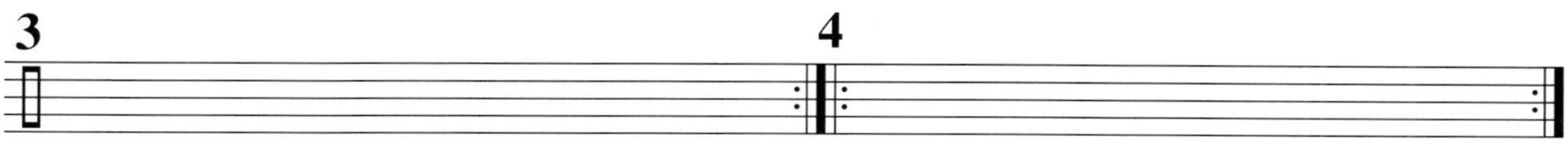

CD 20 0:57

CD 20 1:15

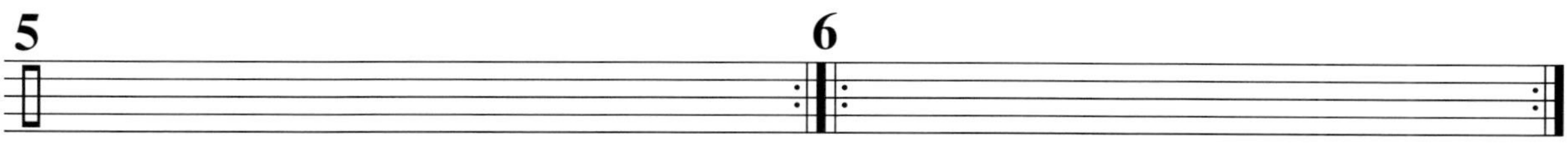

CD 20 1:34

THE ANSWERS ARE ON PAGE 65

Rhythm #9 (prep.)

Rhythm #9 is *based upon* the <u>second and fourth 16th note</u> (of the four 16th notes per beat). This is illustrated below rhythm #9. See figure A.

Rhythm #9 

Figure A 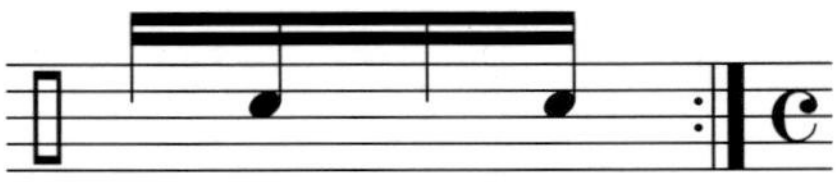

Here is the prep. exercise for rhythm #9 written in 4/4. I recommend that you *play along* with the audio. Make sure to look at rhythm #9 as you play. This will help you to associate the sound of the rhythm with the written notation. Also, notice the relationship between rhythm #9 and the click.

Track 21 

(1) **E** **AH** (2) **E** **AH** (3) **E** **AH** (4) **E** **AH**

All of the beats on this page incorporate rhythm #9 (from page 24). In addition, I will also include the bass drum on beats one and/or three as well as the snare drum on beats two and/or four.

RHYTHM #9

Here is rhythm #9 *combined* with the 8th note cymbal pattern:

(w/bass drum) or (w/snare drum)

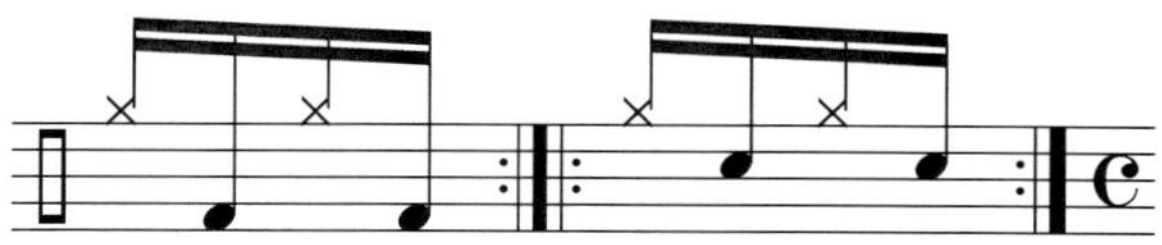

Listen to the audio and transcribe the following beats. Remember to start by writing the 8th note cymbal pattern.

Track 22
EX. 1-6

1 **2**

CD 22 0:00

CD 22 0:19

3 **4**

CD 22 0:37

CD 22 0:56

5 **6**

CD 22 1:14

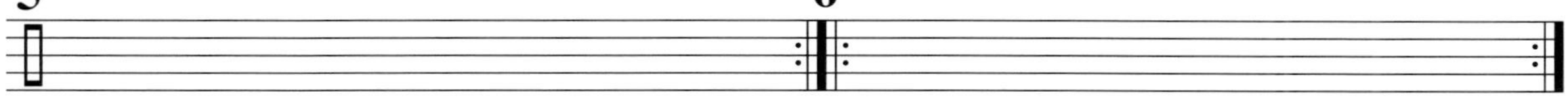

CD 22 1:33

THE ANSWERS ARE ON PAGE 66

Rhythm #10 (prep.)

Rhythm #10 is *based upon* the third and fourth 16th note (of the four 16th notes per beat). This is illustrated below rhythm #10. See figure A.

Rhythm #10 

Figure A 

Here is the prep. exercise for rhythm #10 written in 4/4. I recommend that you *play along* with the audio. Make sure to look at rhythm #10 as you play. This will help you to associ-ate the sound of the rhythm with the written notation. Also, notice the relationship between rhythm #10 and the click.

Track 23 

All of the beats on this page incorporate rhythm #10 (from page 26). *In addition, I will also include the bass drum on beats one and/or three as well as the snare drum on beats two and/or four.*

RHYTHM #10

Here is rhythm #10 *combined* with the 8th note cymbal pattern:

(w/bass drum) or (w/snare drum)

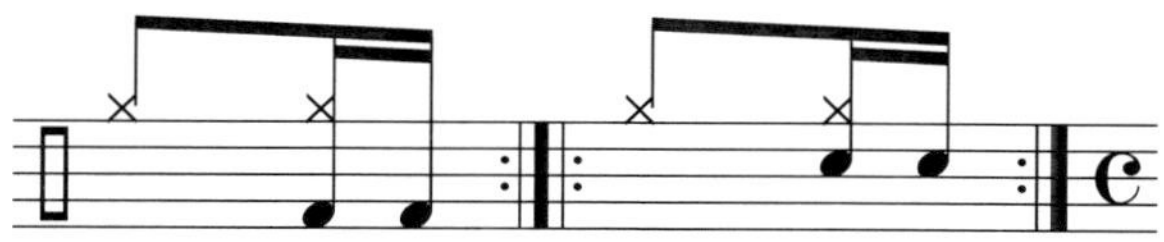

Listen to the audio and transcribe the following beats. Remember to start by writing the 8th note cymbal pattern.

Track 24
EX. 1-6

1 2

CD 24 0:00

CD 24 0:18

3 4

CD 24 0:37

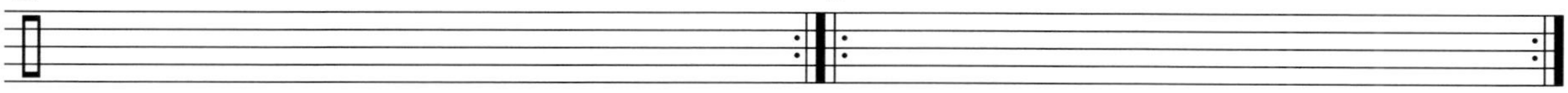

CD 24 0:56

5 6

CD 24 1:15

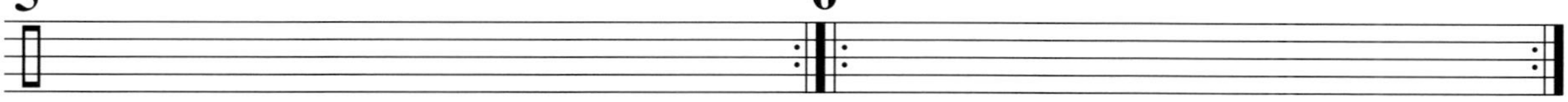

CD 24 1:33

THE ANSWERS ARE ON PAGE 66

Rhythm #11 (prep.)

Rhythm #11 is *based upon* the <u>first, second and third 16th note</u> (of the four 16th notes per beat).This is illustrated below rhythm #11. See figure A.

Rhythm #11 

Figure A 

Here is the prep. exercise for rhythm #11 written in 4/4. I recommend that you *play along* with the audio. Make sure to look at rhythm #11 as you play. This will help you to associ-ate the sound of the rhythm with the written notation. Also, notice the relationship between rhythm #11 and the click.

Track 25

All of the beats on this page incorporate rhythm #11 (from page 28). In addition, I will also include the bass drum on beats one and/or three as well as the snare drum on beats two and/or four.

RHYTHM #11

Here is rhythm #11 *combined* with the 8th note cymbal pattern:

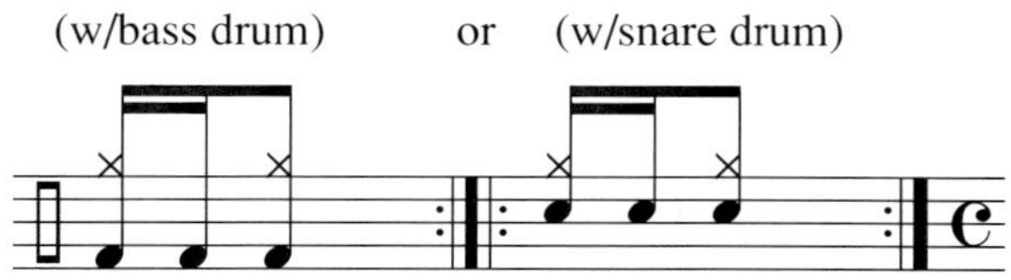

Listen to the audio and transcribe the following beats. Remember to start by writing the 8th note cymbal pattern.

Track 26
EX. 1-6

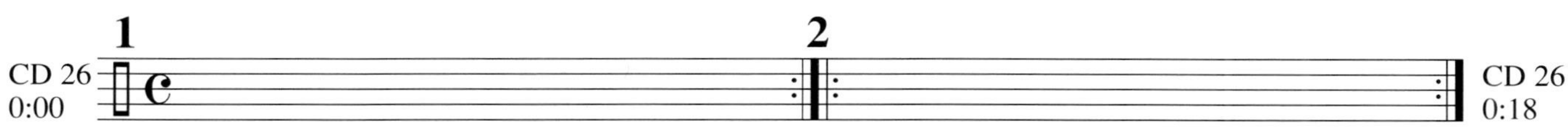

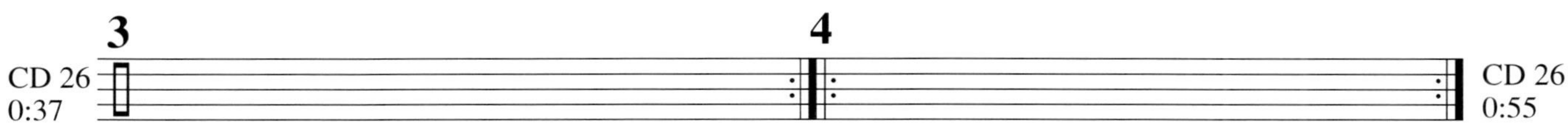

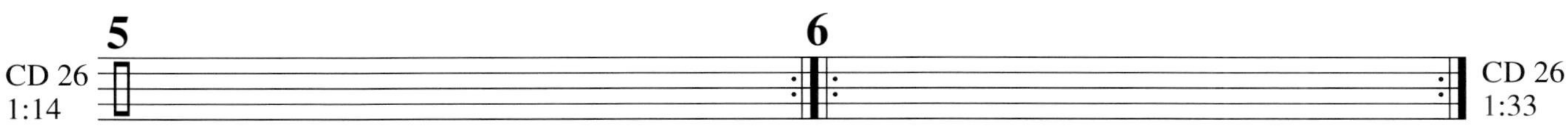

THE ANSWERS ARE ON PAGE 67

Rhythm #12 (prep.)

Rhythm #12 is *based upon* the first, second and third 16th note (of the four 16th notes per beat).This is illustrated below rhythm #12. See figure A.

Rhythm #12 

Figure A 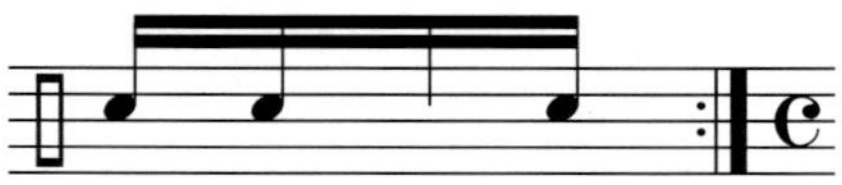

Here is the prep. exercise for rhythm #12 written in 4/4. I recommend that you *play along* with the audio. Make sure to look at rhythm #12 as you play. This will help you to associ-ate the sound of the rhythm with the written notation. Also, notice the relationship between rhythm #12 and the click.

Track 27 

1 E AH 2 E AH 3 E AH 4 E AH

All of the beats on this page incorporate rhythm #12 (from page 30). In addition, I will also include the bass drum on beats one and/or three as well as the snare drum on beats two and/or four.

RHYTHM #12

Here is rhythm #12 *combined* with the 8th note cymbal pattern:

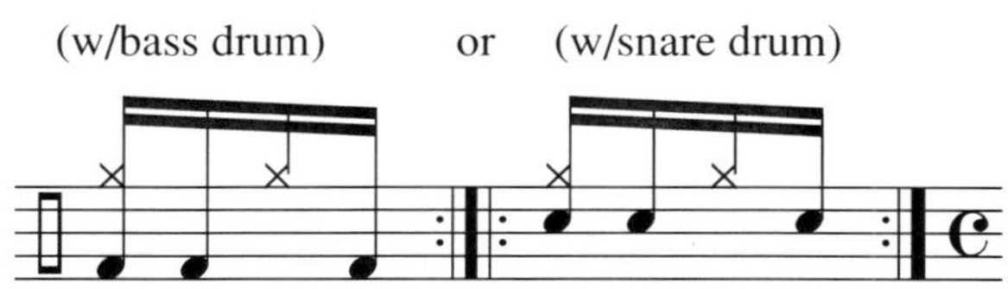

Listen to the audio and transcribe the following beats. Remember to start by writing the 8th note cymbal pattern.

Track 28
EX. 1-6

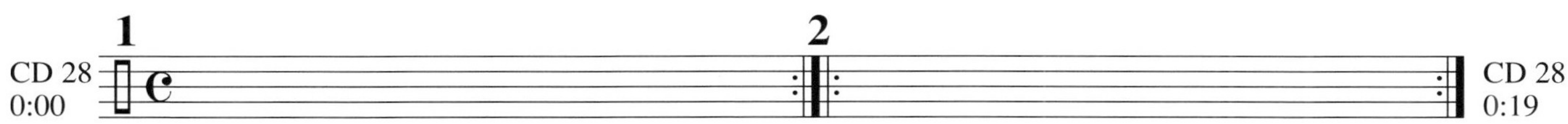

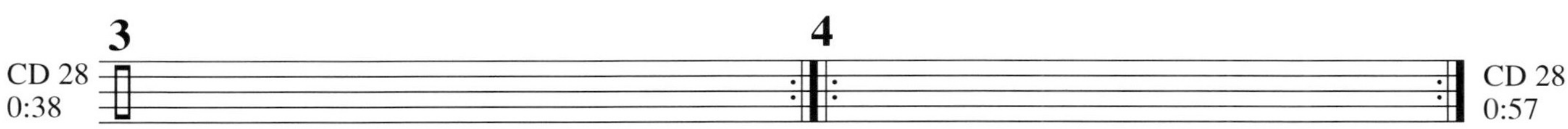

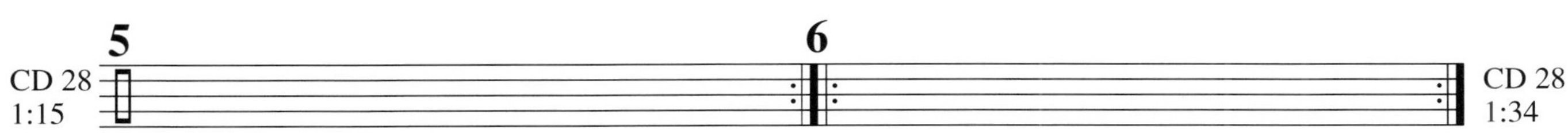

THE ANSWERS ARE ON PAGE 67

Rhythm #13 (prep.)

Rhythm #13 is *based upon* the first, third and fourth 16th note (of the four 16th notes per beat).This is illustrated below rhythm #13. See figure A.

Rhythm #13 

Figure A 

Here is the prep. exercise for rhythm #13 written in 4/4. I recommend that you *play along* with the audio. Make sure to look at rhythm #13 as you play. This will help you to associ-ate the sound of the rhythm with the written notation. Also, notice the relationship between rhythm #13 and the click.

Track 29 

All of the beats on this page incorporate rhythm #13 (from page 32). *In addition, I will also include the bass drum on beats one and/or three as well as the snare drum on beats two and/or four.*

RHYTHM #13

Here is rhythm #13 *combined* with the 8th note cymbal pattern:

(w/bass drum) or (w/snare drum)

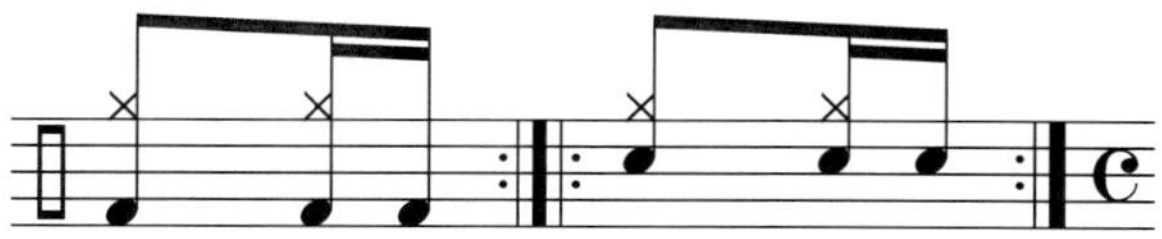

Listen to the audio and transcribe the following beats. Remember to start by writing the 8th note cymbal pattern.

Track 30
EX. 1-6

1 2

CD 30 0:00

CD 30 0:18

3 4

CD 30 0:37

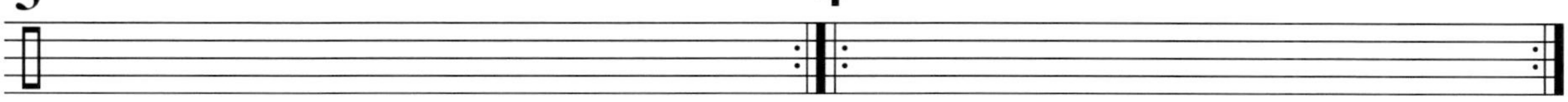

CD 30 0:55

5 6

CD 30 1:14

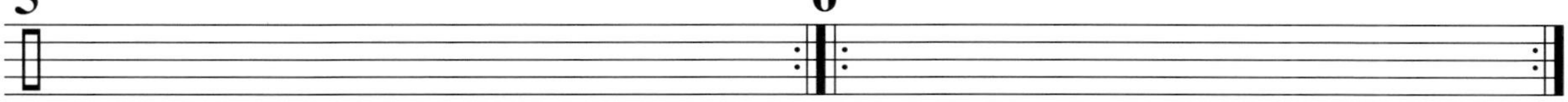

CD 30 1:33

THE ANSWERS ARE ON PAGE 68

Rhythm #14 (prep.)

Rhythm #14 is *based upon* the second, third and fourth 16th note (of the four 16th notes per beat).This is illustrated below rhythm #14. See figure A.

Rhythm #14 

Figure A 

Here is the prep. exercise for rhythm #14 written in 4/4. I recommend that you *play along* with the audio. Make sure to look at rhythm #14 as you play. This will help you to associ-ate the sound of the rhythm with the written notation. Also, notice the relationship between rhythm #14 and the click.

Track 31 

(1) **E & AH** (2) **E & AH** (3) **E & AH** (4) **E & AH**

All of the beats on this page incorporate rhythm #14 (from page 34). *In addition, I will also include the bass drum on beats one and/or three as well as the snare drum on beats two and/or four.*

RHYTHM #14

Here is rhythm #14 *combined* with the 8th note cymbal pattern:

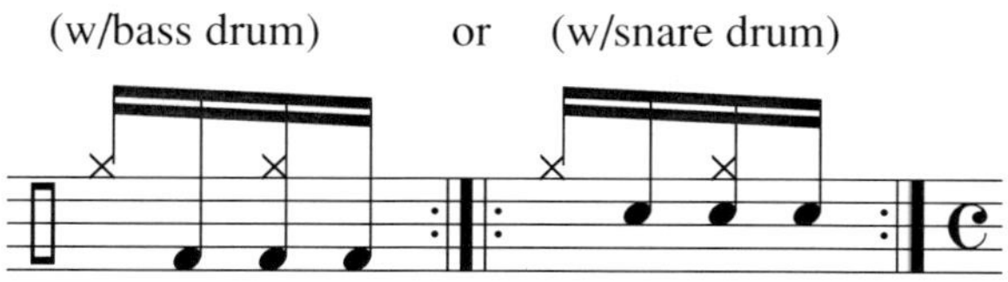

Listen to the audio and transcribe the following beats. Remember to start by writing the 8th note cymbal pattern.

Track 32
EX. 1-6

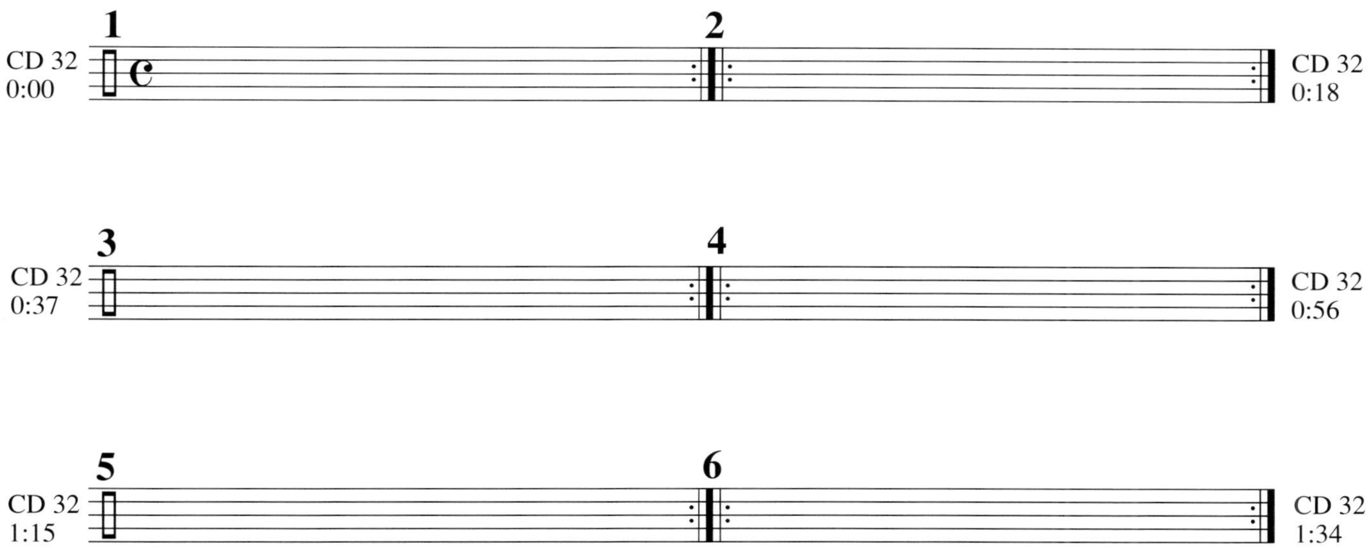

THE ANSWERS ARE ON PAGE 68

Rhythm #15 (prep.)

Rhythm #15 is *based upon* the **first, second, third and fourth 16th note** (of the four 16th notes per beat).This is illustrated below rhythm #15. See figure A.

Rhythm #15 

Figure A 

Here is the prep. exercise for rhythm #15 written in 4/4. I recommend that you *play along* with the audio. Make sure to look at rhythm #15 as you play. This will help you to associ-ate the sound of the rhythm with the written notation. Also, notice the relationship between rhythm #15 and the click.

Track 33 

All of the beats on this page incorporate rhythm #15 (from page 36). *In addition, I will also include the bass drum on beats one and/or three as well as the snare drum on beats two and/or four.*

RHYTHM #15

Here is rhythm #15 *combined* with the 8th note cymbal pattern:

(w/bass drum) or (w/snare drum)

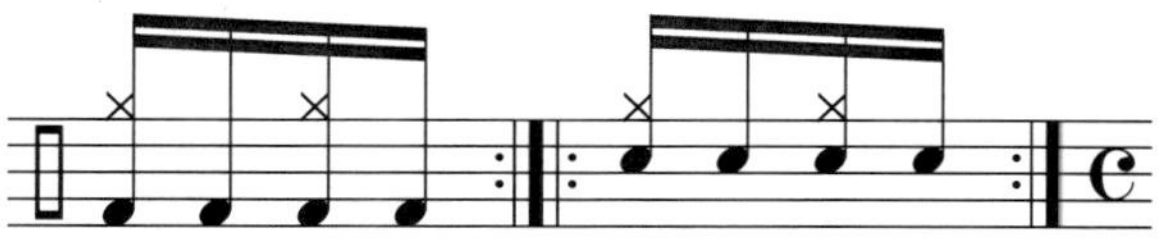

Listen to the audio and transcribe the following beats. Remember to start by writing the 8th note cymbal pattern.

Track 34
EX. 1-6

1 2

CD 34 0:00  CD 34 0:18

3 4

CD 34 0:37 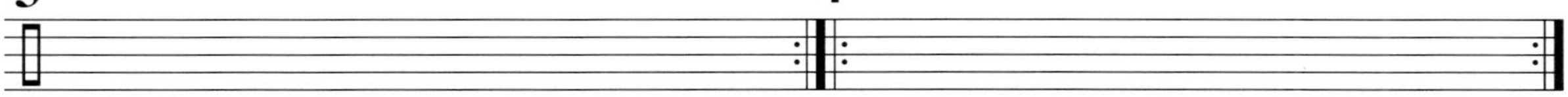 CD 34 0:55

5 6

CD 34 1:14 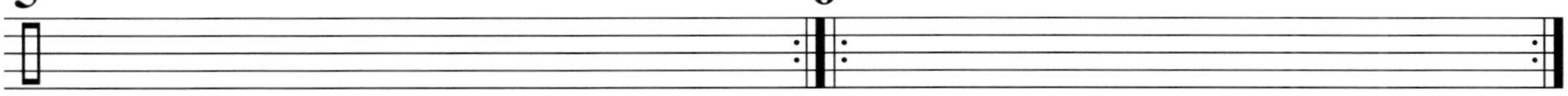 CD 34 1:33

THE ANSWERS ARE ON PAGE 69

Random 16th Combinations

In this section, the hi-hat will once again play 8th notes. However, the bass and snare will play the 16th note variations in *random order*. Remember to start by writing the 8th note cymbal pattern.

Track 35
EX. 1-6

Listen to the audio and transcribe the following beats.

1

CD 35
0:00

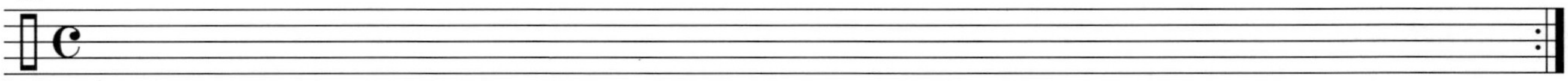

2

CD 35
0:18

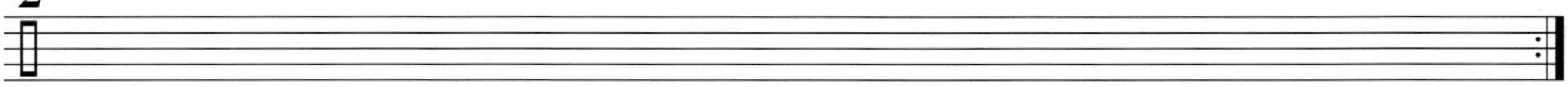

3

CD 35
0:36

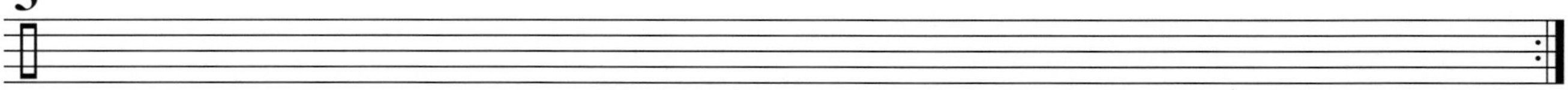

4

CD 35
0:55

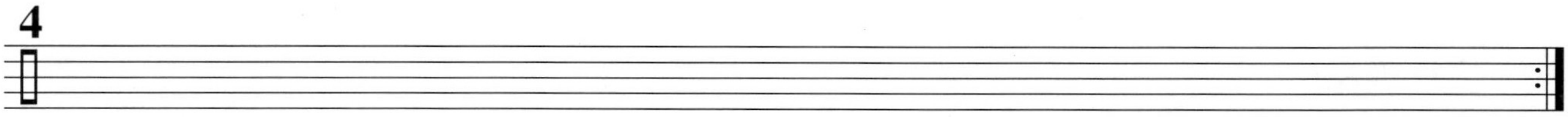

5

CD 35
1:13

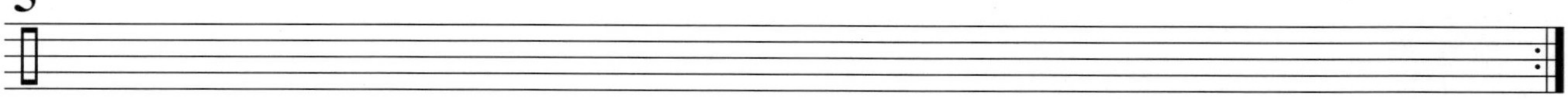

6

CD 35
1:32

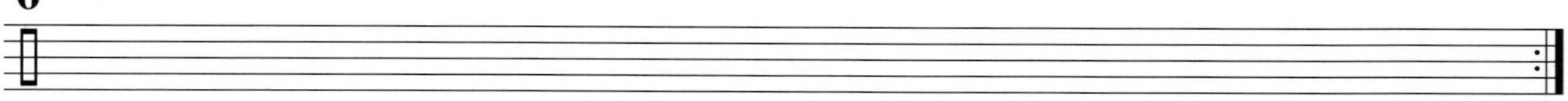

THE ANSWERS ARE ON PAGE 70

Random 16th Combinations Continued

Listen to the audio and transcribe the following beats.

Track 36
EX. 1-6

1

CD 36
0:00

2

CD 36
0:18

3

CD 36
0:36

4

CD 36
0:54

5

CD 36
1:13

6

CD 36
1:32

THE ANSWERS ARE ON PAGE 71

Random Hi-Hat Combinations

Now it's time to (randomly) apply rhythms 1-15 on the hi-hat. All of the following grooves will use the same bass drum and snare drum pattern (A). I recommend that you write out this pattern now on examples 2-6. I have provided example 1 for you.

Track 37

Listen to the audio and transcribe the following beats.

Track 38
EX. 1-6

CD 38 0:00

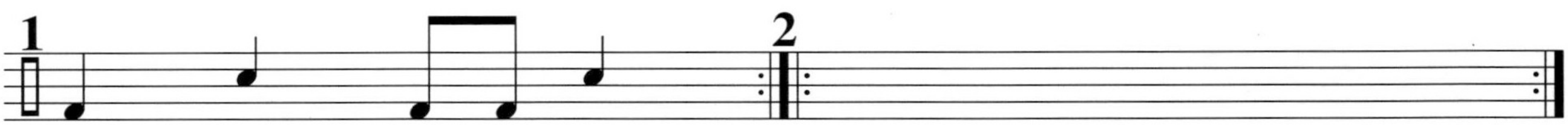

CD 38 0:18

CD 38 0:37

CD 38 0:55

CD 38 1:13

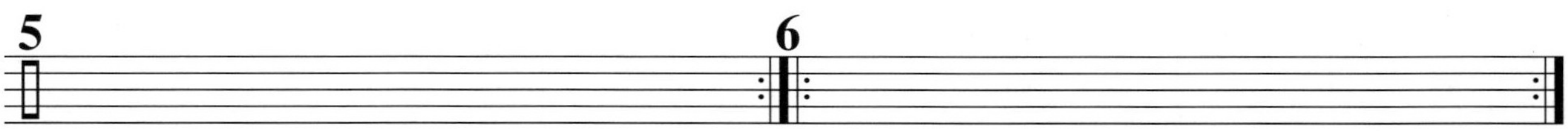

CD 38 1:32

THE ANSWERS ARE ON PAGE 72

Random Combinations
(Everything)

In this section I'm taking away the *training wheels*. In other words, the following examples combine the 16th note variations in random order to the ***bass, snare and hi-hat.*** Good luck! Listen to the audio and transcribe the following beats.

Track 39
EX. 1-6

1

CD 39
0:00

2

CD 39
0:19

3

CD 39
0:37

4

CD 39
0:56

5

CD 39
1:14

6

CD 39
1:33

THE ANSWERS ARE ON PAGE 73

Random Fills

In this section, we will focus on fills that use the 16th note variations in random order. Each fill will be one bar long preceeded by the following basic rock beat. **Hint:** If you need help, refer to the prep. exercises on pages 8-36 (even numbered pages).

Track 40
EX. 1-9

1 CD 40 0:00

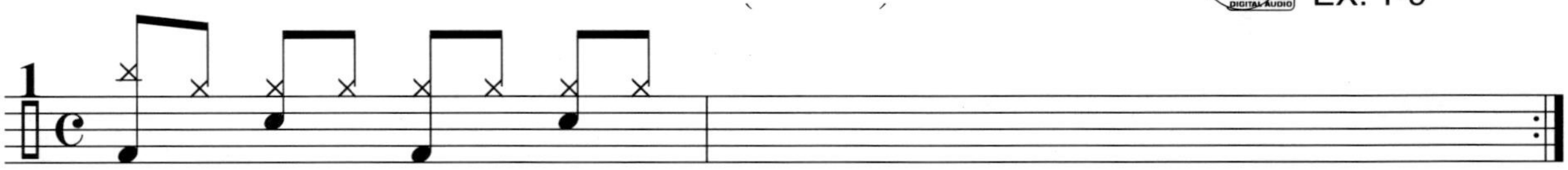

2 CD 40 0:33

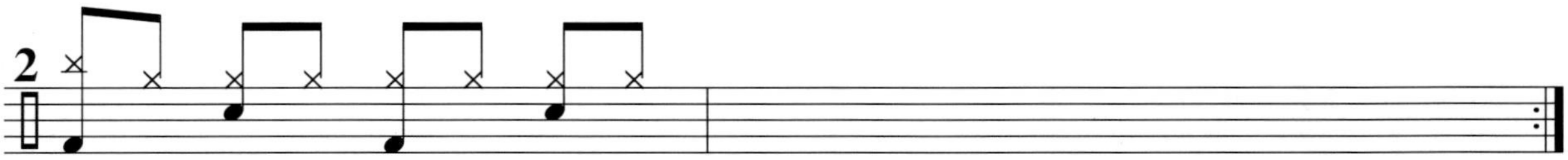

3 CD 40 1:06

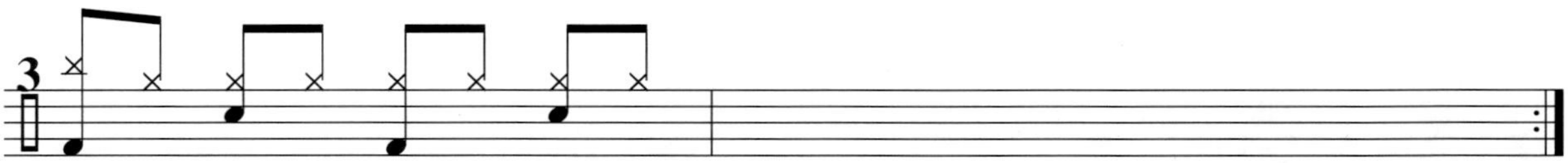

4 CD 40 1:39

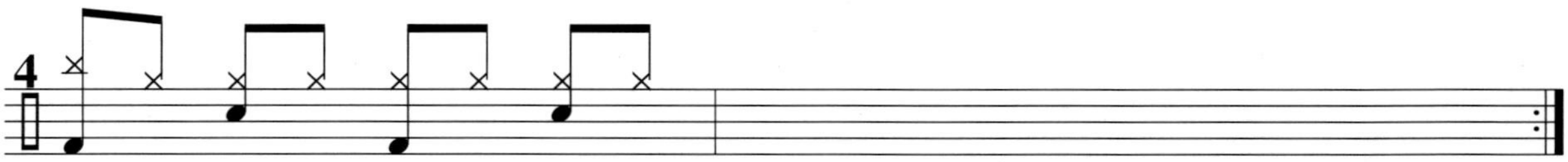

5 CD 40 2:12

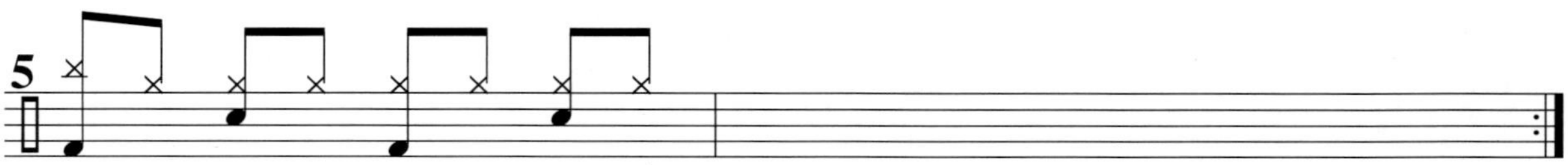

6 CD 40 2:45

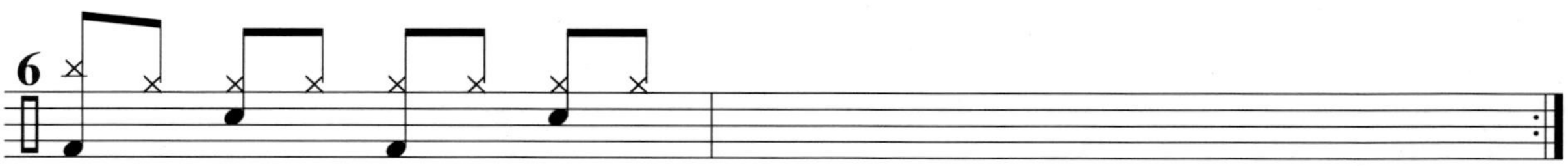

7 CD 40 3:18

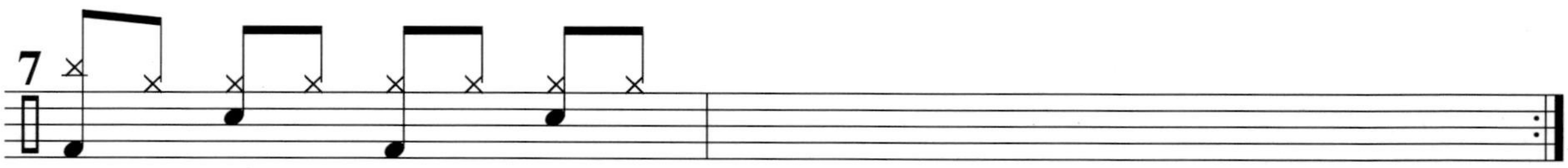

8 CD 40 3:50

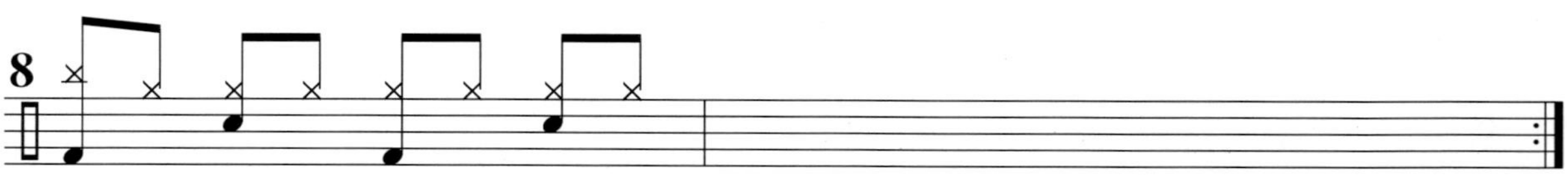

9 CD 40 4:23

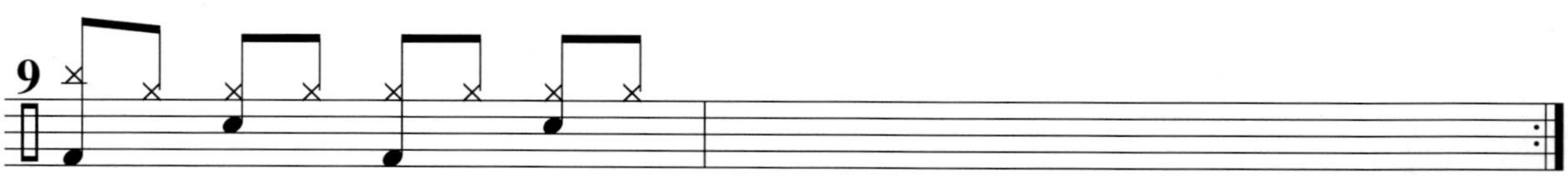

THE ANSWERS ARE ON PAGE 74

Pre-section Two

(8th note)

Triplets

In section two we are going to transcribe beats and fills based upon 8th note triplets. **Before we get started,** let's learn how to read, write and play 8th note triplets.

Turn on your metronome to any speed (I recommend starting slow). Play *three* evenly spaced hits (per click) along with your metronome. You are now playing 8th note triplets.

Here is the written notation for 8th note triplets:

Track 41

Section Two

Triplet Feel

All of the beats in section 2 (pages 45-58) will use the following eighth note triplet hi-hat rhythm. Let's play along! This will help you to become familiar with this ryhthm.

Track 42

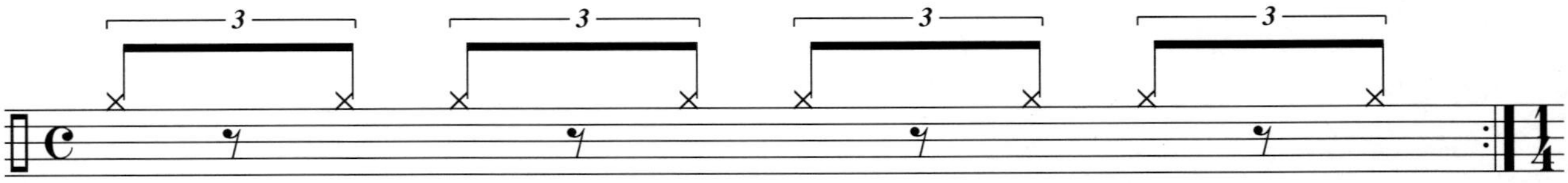

We will learn to incorporate <u>one rhythm at a time</u> *along* with the above hi-hat rhythm. The (seven) rhythms you are about to learn are subdivisions of eighth note triplets.

Rhythm #1 (prep.)

Rhythm #1 is *based upon* the <u>first 8th note</u> (of the three 8th note triplets per beat). This is illustrated below rhythm #1. See figure A.

Rhythm #1

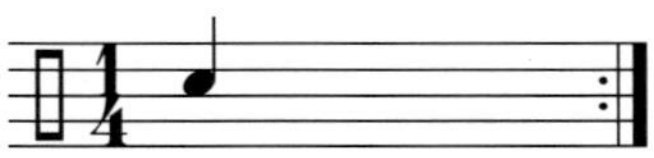

Figure A

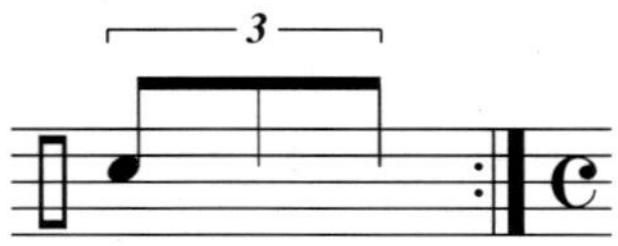

Here is the prep. exercise for rhythm #1 written in 4/4. I recommend that you *play along* with with the audio. Also, make sure to look at rhythm #1 as you play. This will help you to associate the sound of the rhythm with the written notation. Notice that this rhythm hits at the same time as the click (metronome).

Track 43

In this section, all of the beats will use the following 8th note triplet cymbal pattern. I recommend that you write out this cymbal rhythm on examples 2-6 now. I have provided example #1 for you.

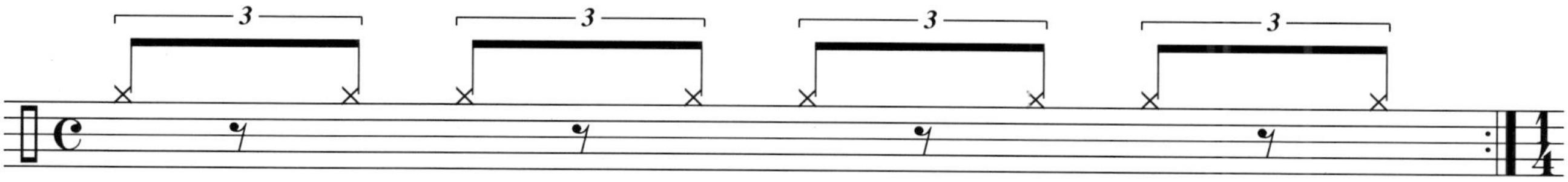

All of the beats on this page incorporate rhythm #1 (from page 44).

RHYTHM #1

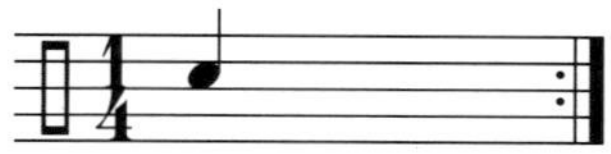

Here is rhythm #1 *combined* with the above cymbal pattern:

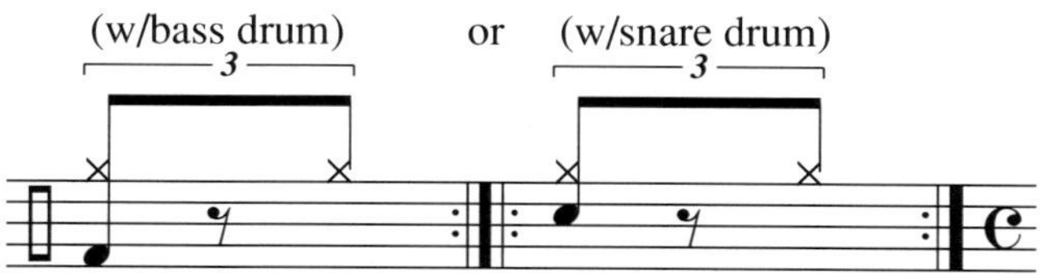

*Listen to the audio and transcribe the following beats.

Track 44
EX. 1-6

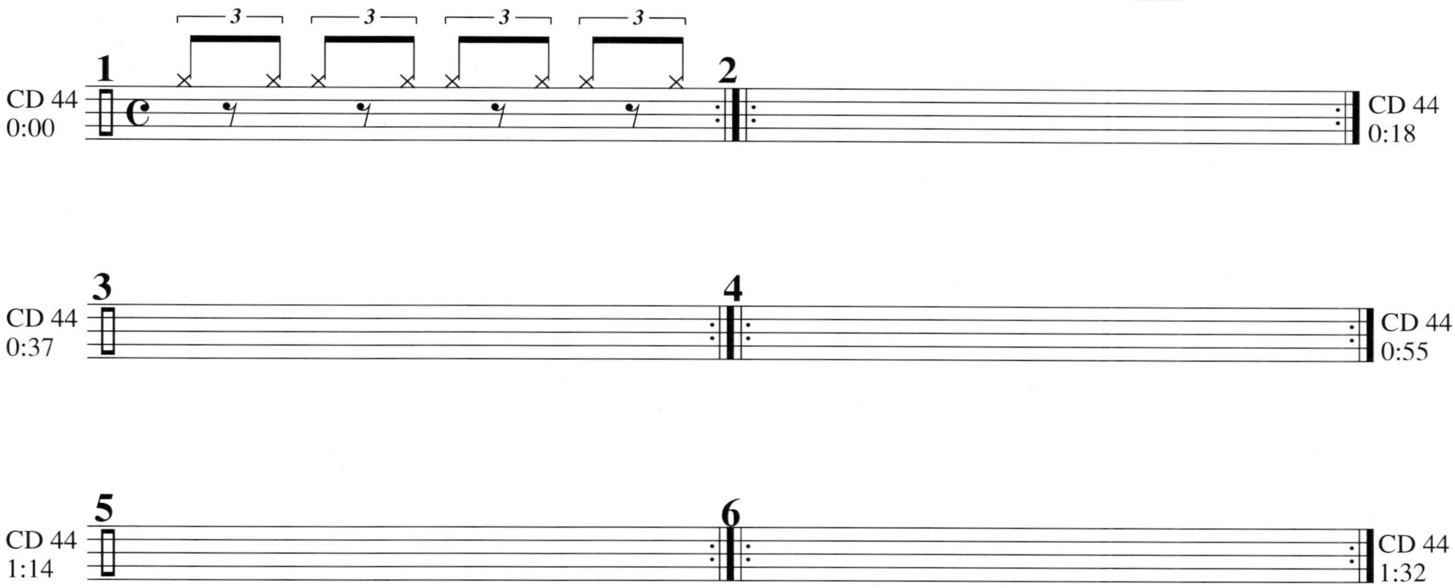

THE ANSWERS ARE ON PAGE 75

Rhythm #2 (prep.)

Rhythm #2 is *based upon* the second 8th note triplet (of the three 8th note triplets per beat).This is illustrated below rhythm #2. See figure A.

Rhythm #2

Figure A

Here is the prep. exercise for rhythm #2 written in 4/4. I recommend that you *play along* with the audio. Make sure to look at rhythm #2 as you play. This will help you to associate the sound of the rhythm with the written notation. Also, notice the relationship between rhythm #2 and the click.

Track 45

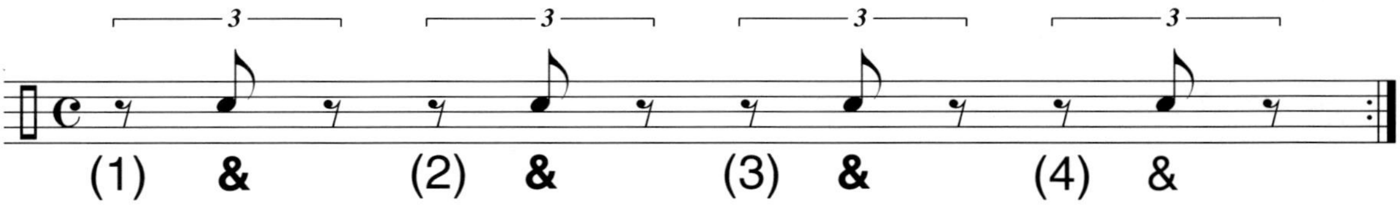

All of the beats on this page incorporate rhythm #2 (from page 46). *In addition, I will also include the bass drum on beats one and/or three as well as the snare drum on beats two and/or four.*

RHYTHM #2

Here is rhythm #2 *combined* with the 8th note cymbal pattern:

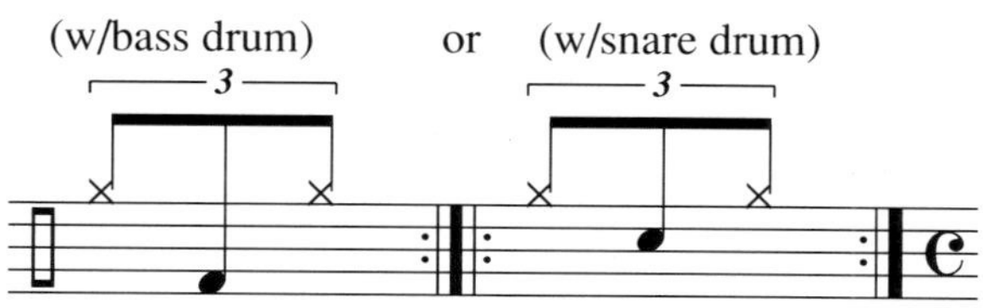

Listen to the audio and transcribe the following beats. Remember to start by writing the 8th note triplet cymbal pattern. Once again, I have provided example 1 for you.*

Track 46
EX. 1-6

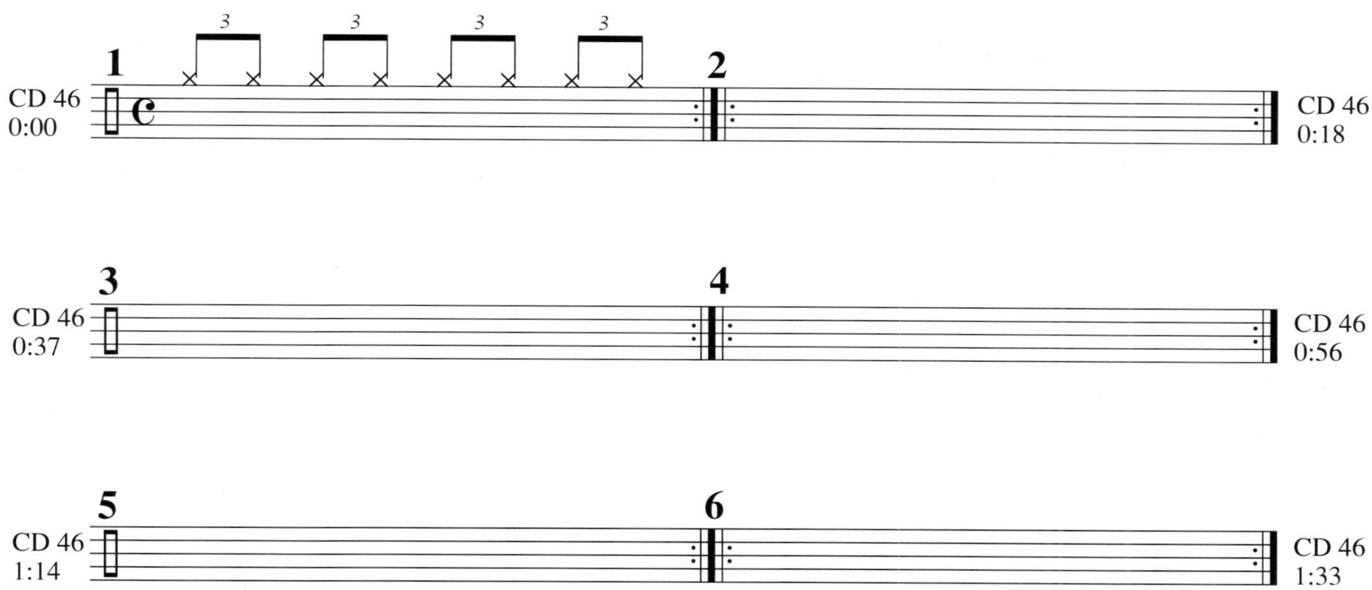

THE ANSWERS ARE ON PAGE 75

* Notice that example #1 does not include 8th note rests on the middle note of each triplet.This will eliminate the need to erase when you are writing beats that utilize rhythm #2. Make sure to include the 8th note rest wherever necessary.

Rhythm #3 (prep.)

Rhythm #3 is *based upon* the **third 8th note triplet** (of the three 8th note triplets per beat).This is illustrated below rhythm #3. See figure A.

Rhythm #3

Figure A

Here is the prep. exercise for rhythm #3 written in 4/4. I recommend that you p*lay along* with the audio. Make sure to look at rhythm #3 as you play. This will help you to associate the sound of the rhythm with the written notation. Also, notice the relationship between rhythm #3 and the click.

Track 47

All of the beats on this page incorporate rhythm #3 (from page 48). *In addition, I will also include the bass drum on beats one and/or three as well as the snare drum on beats two and/or four.*

RHYTHM #3

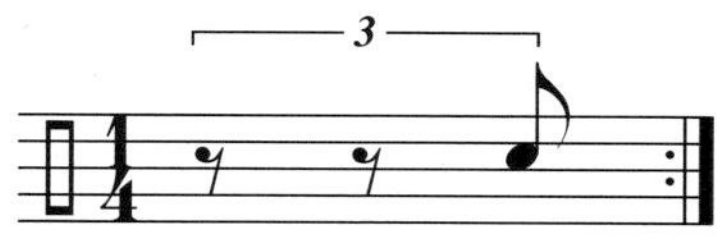

Here is rhythm #3 *combined* with the 8th note cymbal pattern:

(w/bass drum) or (w/snare drum)

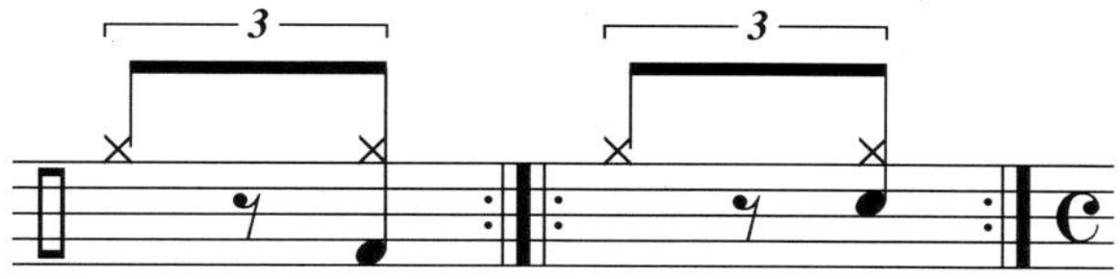

Listen to the audio and transcribe the following beats. Remember to start by writing the 8th note triplet cymbal pattern.

Track 48
EX. 1-6

1 2

CD 48 0:00

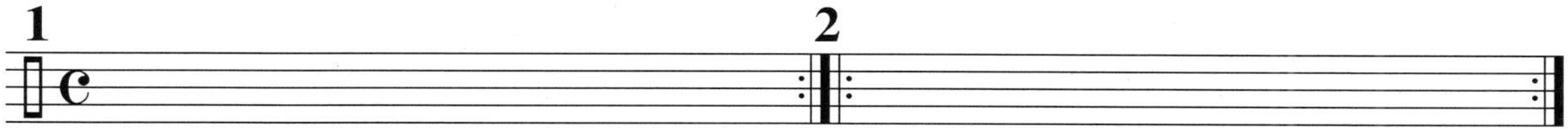

CD 48 0:18

3 4

CD 48 0:37

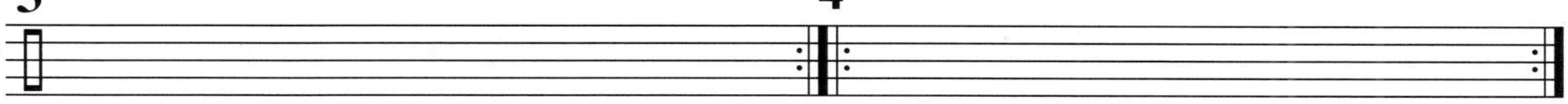

CD 48 0:56

5 6

CD 48 1:15

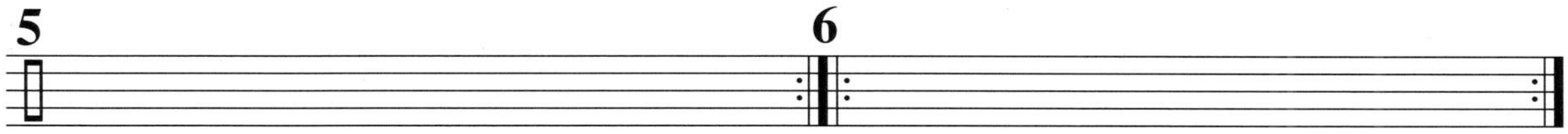

CD 48 1:34

THE ANSWERS ARE ON PAGE 76

Rhythm #4 (prep.)

Rhythm #4 is *based upon* the first and second 8th note triplet (of the three 8th note triplets per beat).This is illustrated below rhythm #4. See figure A.

Rhythm #4

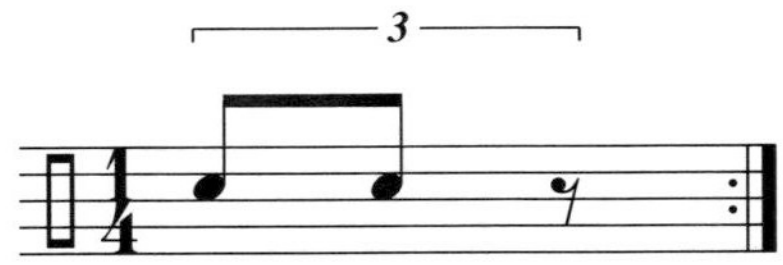

Figure A

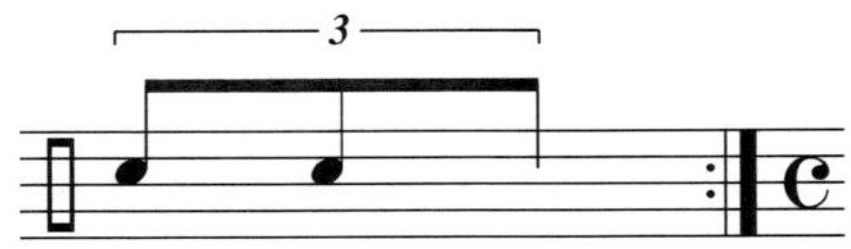

Here is the prep. exercise for rhythm #4 written in 4/4. I recommend that you *play along* with the audio. Make sure to look at rhythm #4 as you play. This will help you to associate the sound of the rhythm with the written notation. Also, notice the relationship between rhythm #4 and the click.

Track 49

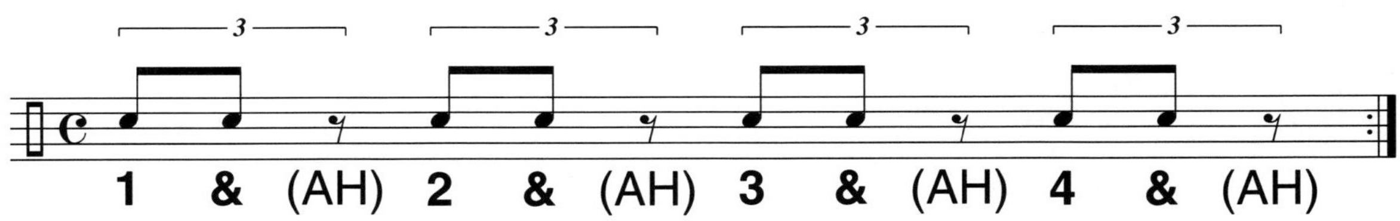

All of the beats on this page incorporate rhythm #4 (from page 50). *In addition, I will also include the bass drum on beats one and/or three as well as the snare drum on beats two and/or four.*

RHYTHM #4

Here is rhythm #4 *combined* with the 8th note cymbal pattern:

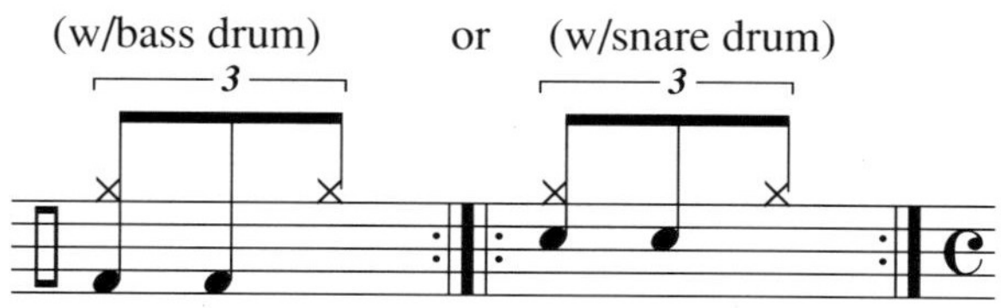

Listen to the audio and transcribe the following beats. Remember to start by writing the 8th note triplet cymbal pattern.

Track 50
EX. 1-6

CD 50 0:00

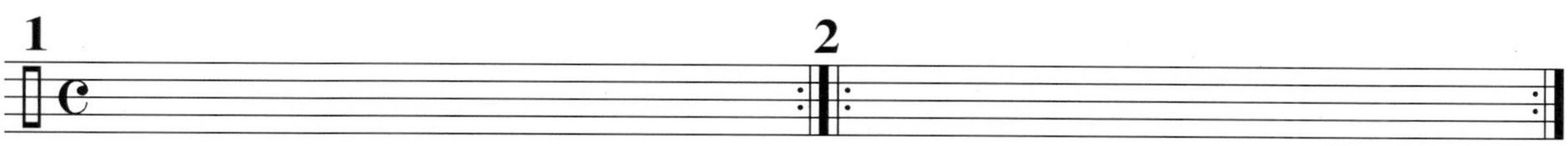

CD 50 0:18

CD 50 0:36

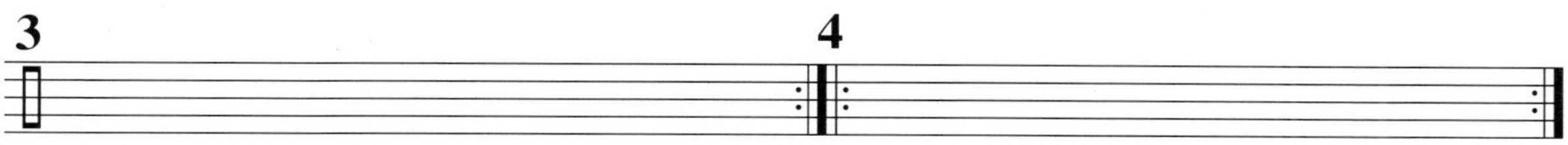

CD 50 0:55

CD 50 1:14

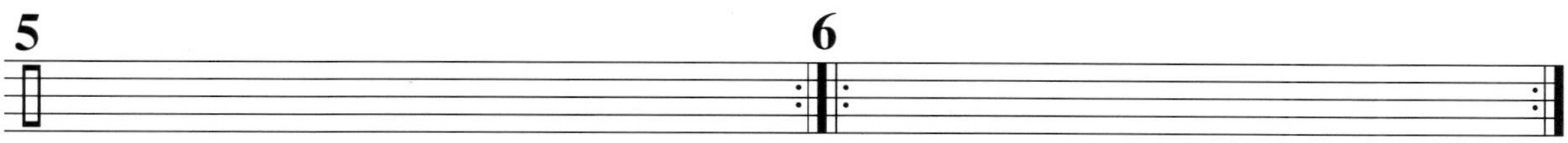

CD 50 1:33

THE ANSWERS ARE ON PAGE 76

Rhythm #5 (prep.)

Rhythm #5 is *based upon* the first and second 8th note triplet (of the three 8th note triplets per beat).This is illustrated below rhythm #5. See figure A.

Rhythm #5

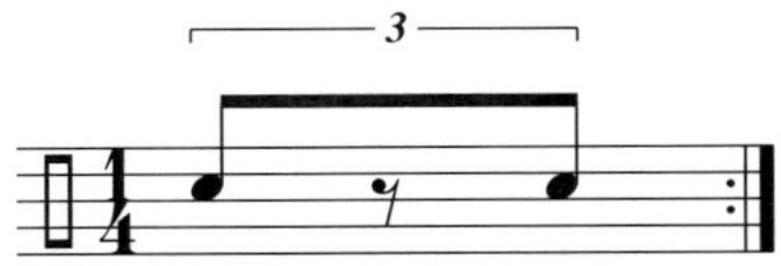

Figure A

Here is the prep. exercise for rhythm #5 written in 4/4. I recommend that you *play along* with the audio. Make sure to look at rhythm #5 as you play. This will help you to associate the sound of the rhythm with the written notation. Also, notice the relationship between rhythm #5 and the click.

Track 51

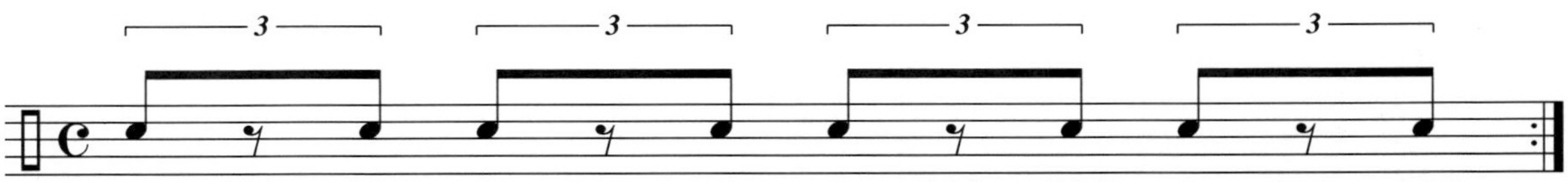

1 (&) AH 2 (&) AH 3 (&) AH 4 (&) AH

All of the beats on this page incorporate rhythm #5 (from page 52). *In addition, I will also include the bass drum on beats one and/or three as well as the snare drum on beats two and/or four.*

RHYTHM #5

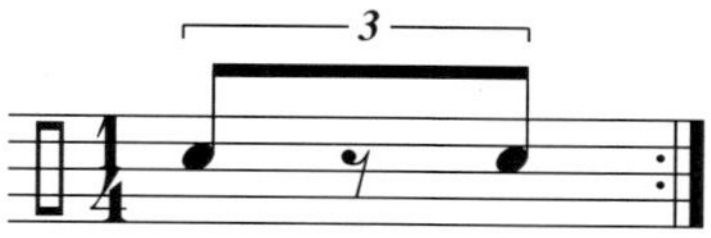

Here is rhythm #5 *combined* with the 8th note cymbal pattern:

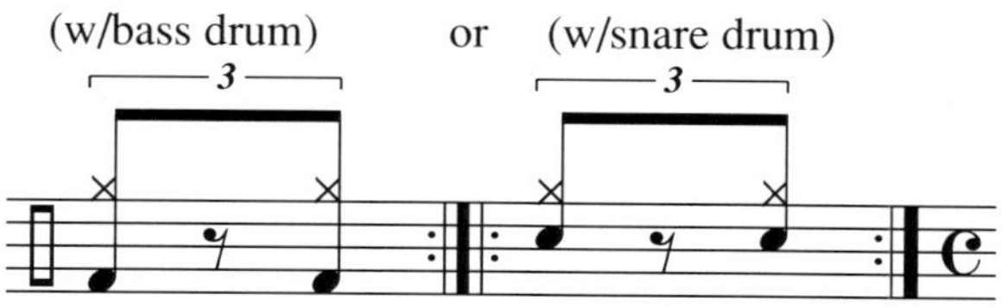

Listen to the audio and transcribe the following beats. Remember to start by writing the 8th note triplet cymbal pattern.

Track 52
EX. 1-6

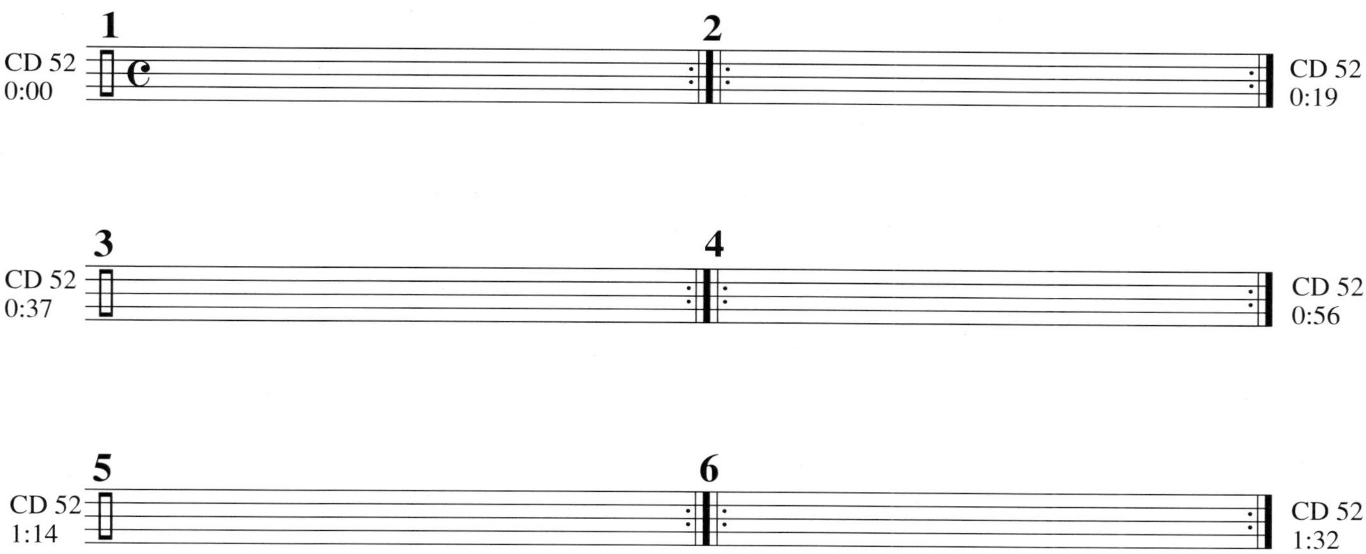

THE ANSWERS ARE ON PAGE 77

Rhythm #6 (prep.)

Rhythm #6 is *based upon* the first and second 8th note triplet (of the three 8th note triplets per beat).This is illustrated below rhythm #6. See figure A.

Rhythm #6

Figure A

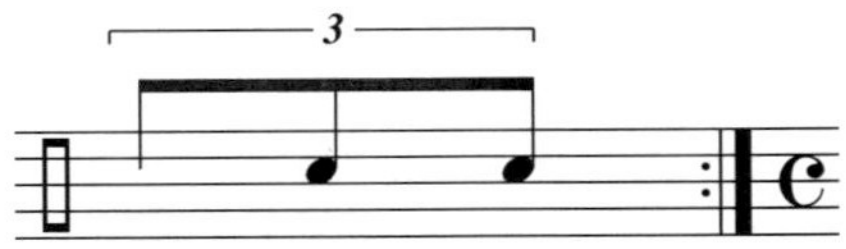

Here is the prep. exercise for rhythm #6 written in 4/4. I recommend that you *play along* with the audio. Make sure to look at rhythm #6 as you play. This will help you to associate the sound of the rhythm with the written notation. Also, notice the relationship between rhythm #6 and the click.

Track 53

(1) **& AH** (2) **& AH** (3) **& AH** (4) **& AH**

All of the beats on this page incorporate rhythm #6 (from page 54). *In addition, I will also include the bass drum on beats one and/or three as well as the snare drum on beats two and/or four.*

RHYTHM #6

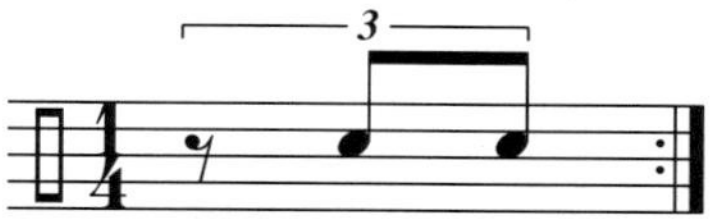

Here is rhythm #6 *combined* with the 8th note cymbal pattern:

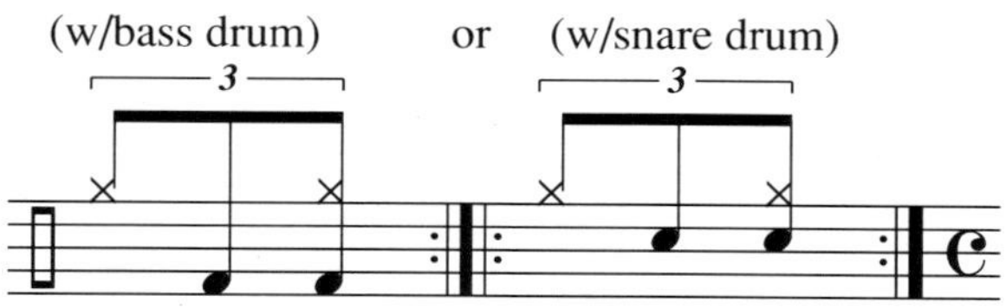

Listen to the audio and transcribe the following beats. Remember to start by writing the 8th note triplet cymbal pattern.

Track 54
EX. 1-6

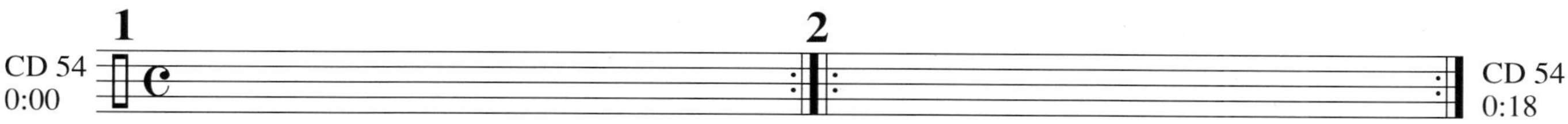

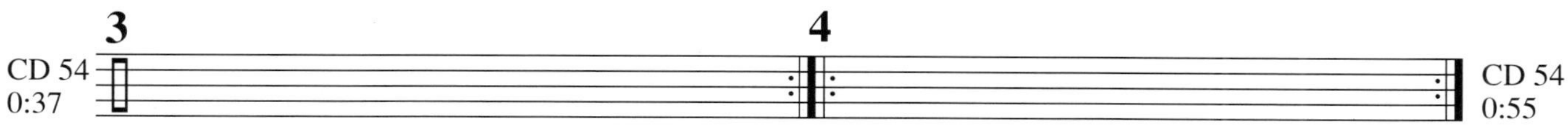

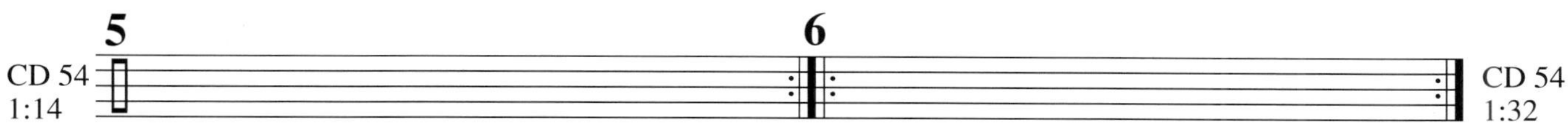

THE ANSWERS ARE ON PAGE 77

Rhythm #7 (prep.)

Rhythm #7 is *based upon* the first and second 8th note triplet (of the three 8th note triplets per beat).This is illustrated below rhythm #7. See figure A.

Rhythm #7

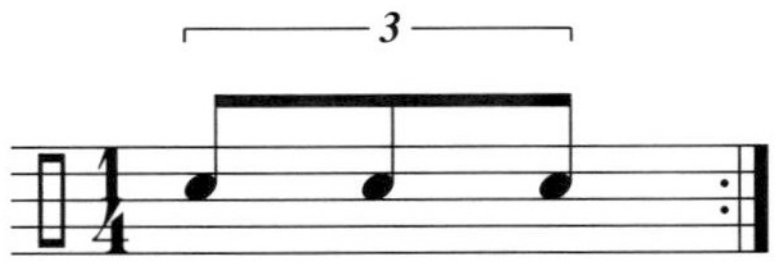

Figure A

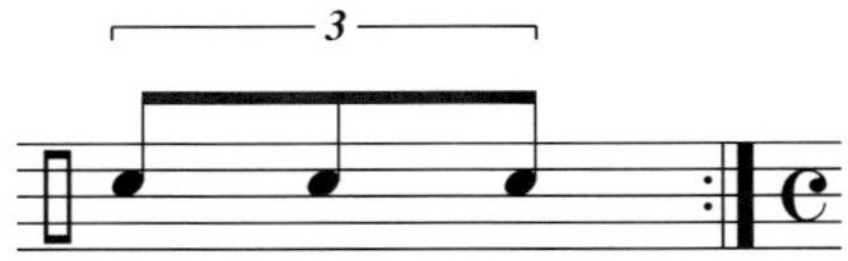

Here is the prep. exercise for rhythm #7 written in 4/4. I recommend that you *play along* with the audio. Make sure to look at rhythm #7 as you play. This will help you to associate the sound of the rhythm with the written notation. Also, notice the relationship between rhythm #7 and the click.

Track 55

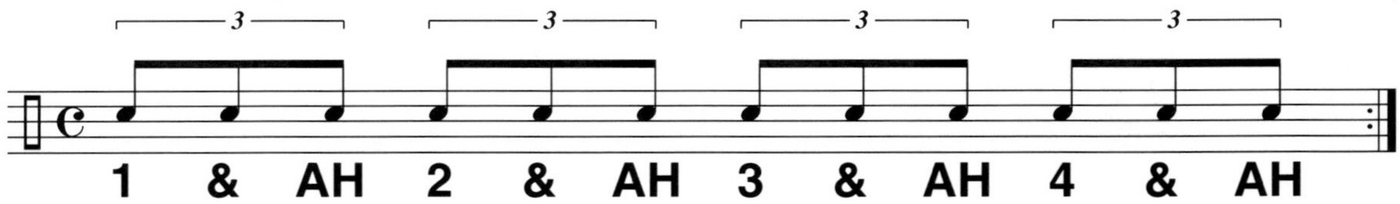

All of the beats on this page incorporate rhythm #7 (from page 56). *In addition, I will also include the bass drum on beats one and/or three as well as the snare drum on beats two and/or four.*

RHYTHM #7

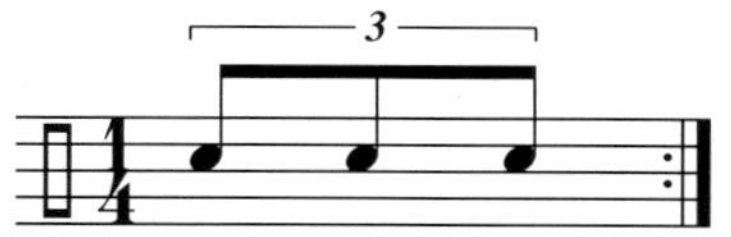

Here is rhythm #7 *combined* with the 8th note cymbal pattern:

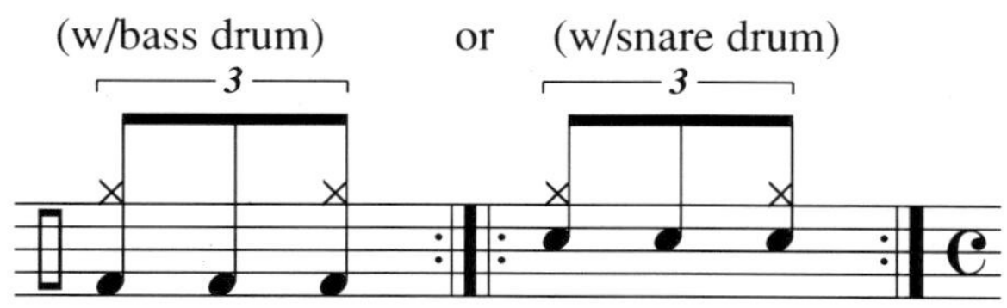

Listen to the audio and transcribe the following beats. Remember to start by writing the 8th note triplet cymbal pattern.

Track 56
EX. 1-6

CD 56 0:00

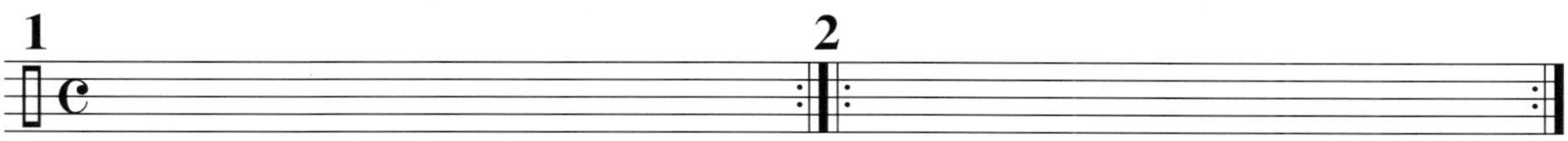

CD 56 0:18

CD 56 0:37

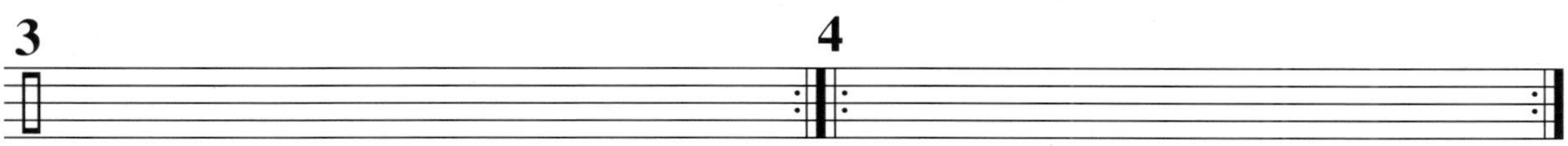

CD 56 0:56

CD 56 1:15

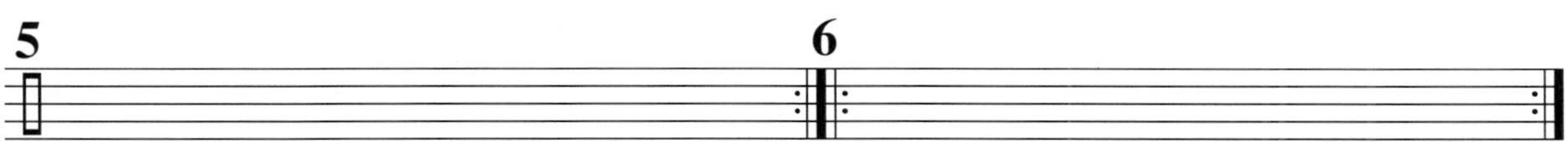

CD 56 1:33

THE ANSWERS ARE ON PAGE 78

Random Triplet Combinations

In this section, the hi-hat will once again play the following 8th note triplet pattern. However, the bass and snare will play the triplet variations (1-7) in random order.

Listen to the audio and transcribe the following beats. Remember to start by writing the cymbal pattern.

Track 57
EX. 1-6

1
CD 57
0:00

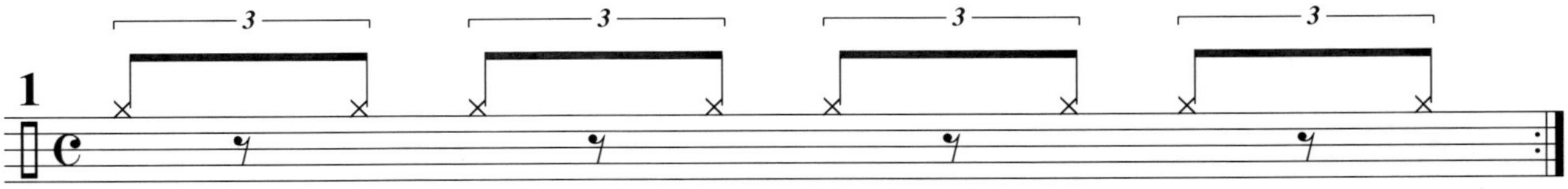

2
CD 57
0:18

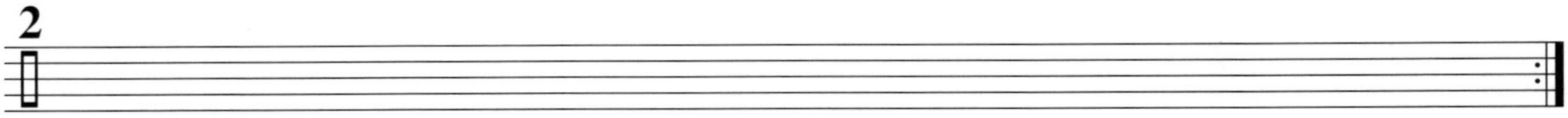

3
CD 57
0:37

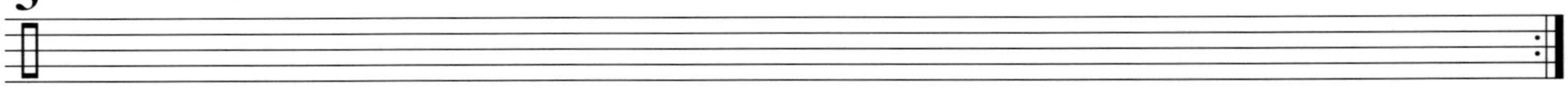

4
CD 57
0:55

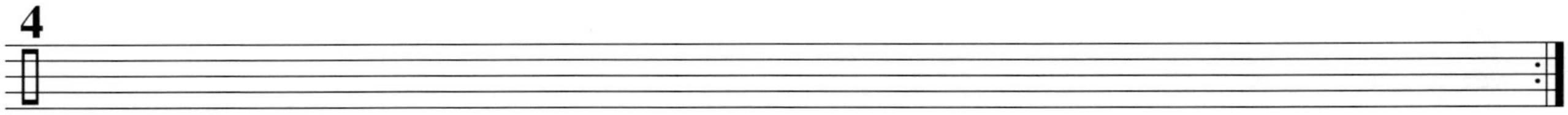

5
CD 57
1:14

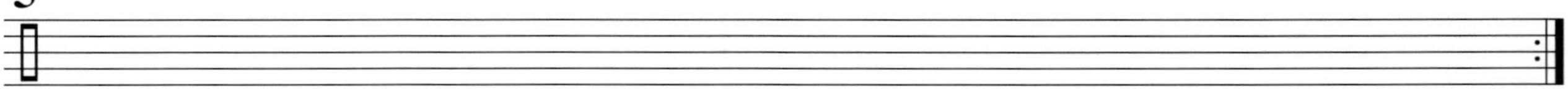

6
CD 57
1:33

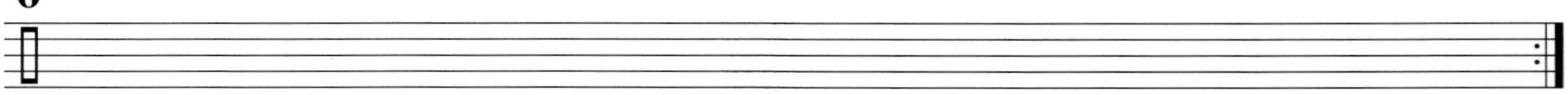

THE ANSWERS ARE ON PAGE 79

Random Hi-Hat Combinations

Now it's time to apply rhythms 1-7 in *random order* on the hi-hat. All of the following grooves will use the same bass drum and snare drum pattern (A). I recommend that you write out this pattern now on examples 2-6. I have provided example 1 for you.

Track 58

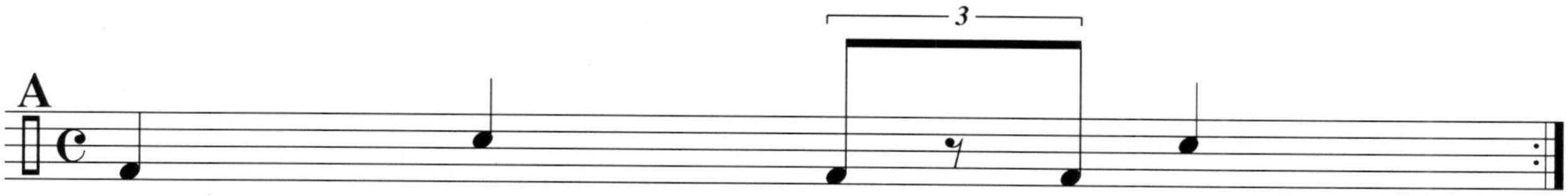

Listen to the audio and transcribe the following beats.

Track 59
EX. 1-6

CD 59 0:00

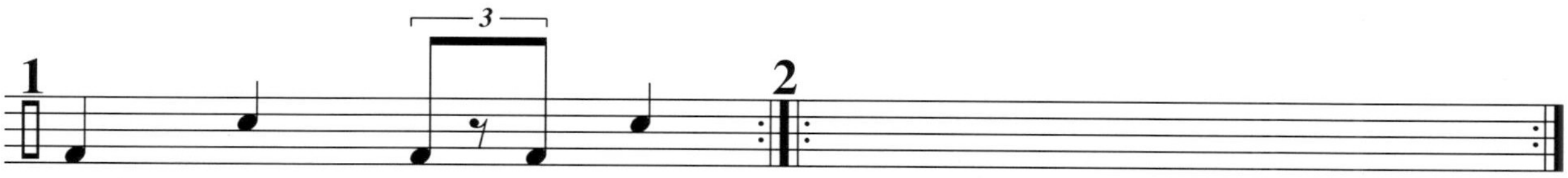

CD 59 0:18

CD 59 0:37

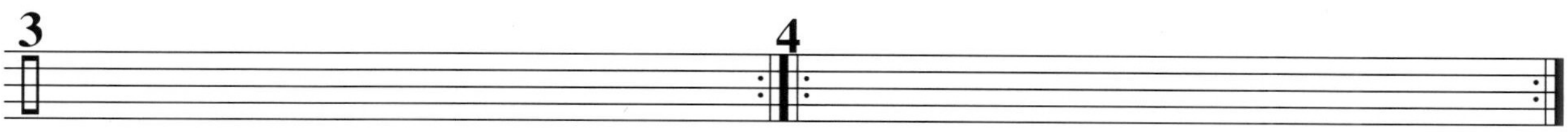

CD 59 0:56

CD 59 1:15

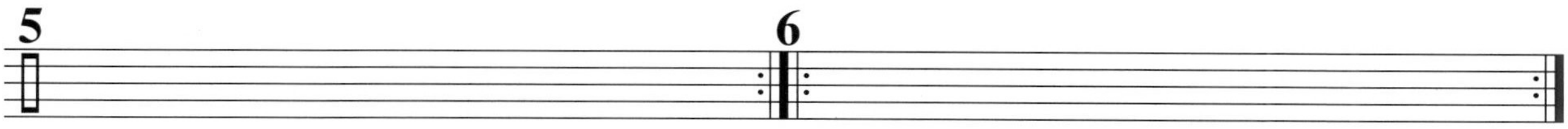

CD 59 1:34

THE ANSWERS ARE ON PAGE 80

Random Combinations

(Everything)

Track 60
EX. 1-6

Once again it's time to take away the *training wheels*. The following examples combine the 8th note triplet variations in random order to the *bass, snare and hi- hat.* Have fun!

1

CD 60
0:00

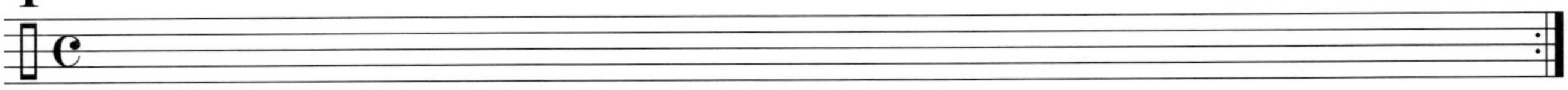

2

CD 60
0:19

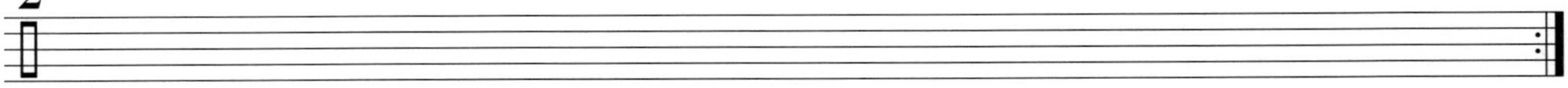

3

CD 60
0:37

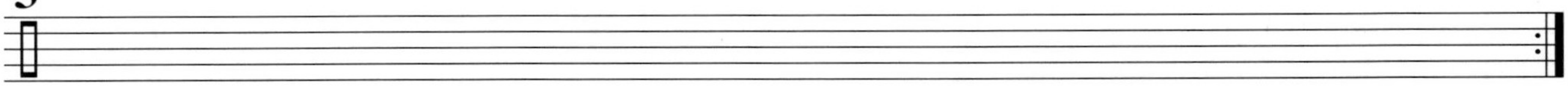

4

CD 60
0:56

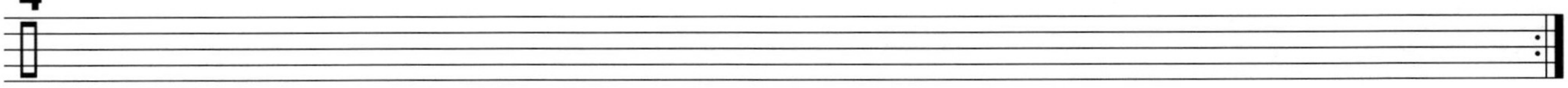

5

CD 60
1:15

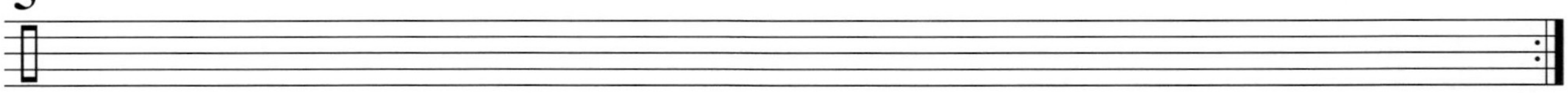

6

CD 60
1:34

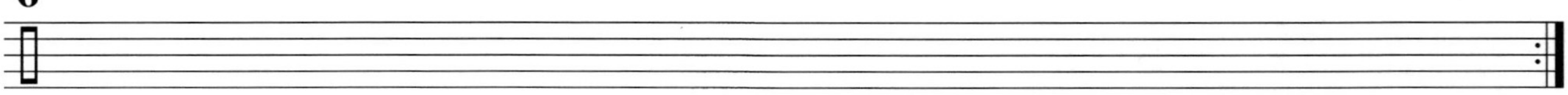

THE ANSWERS ARE ON PAGE 81

Random Triplet Fills

Track 61
EX. 1-9

In this section, we will focus on fills that use the triplet variations in random order. Each fill will be one bar long preceeded by the following basic shuffle. **Hint:** If you need help, refer to the prep. exercises starting on pages 44-56 (even numbered pages).

1
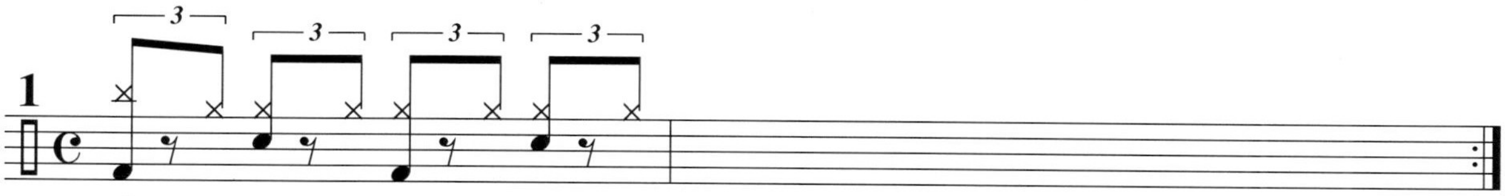
CD 61
0:00

2
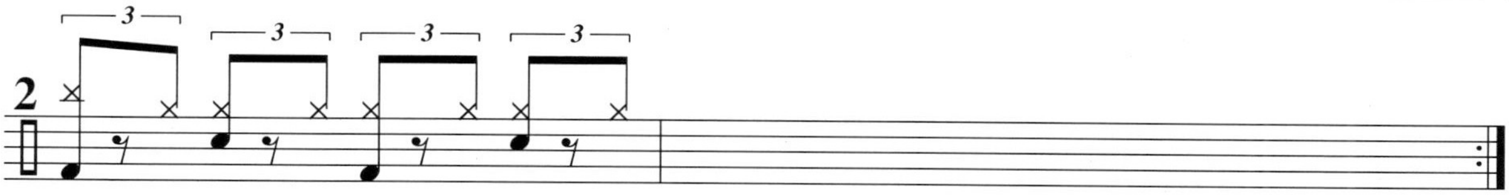
CD 61
0:32

3
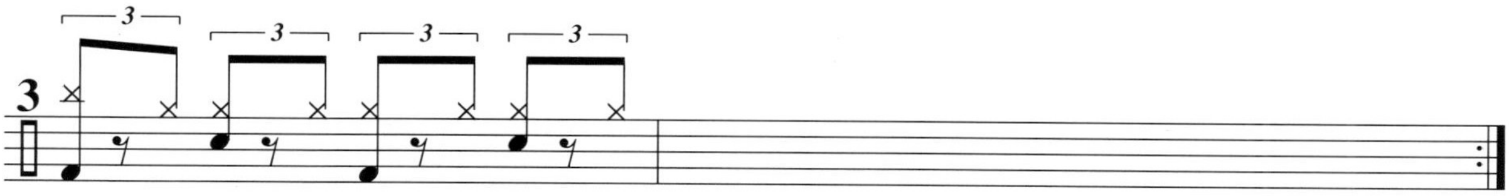
CD 61
1:05

4
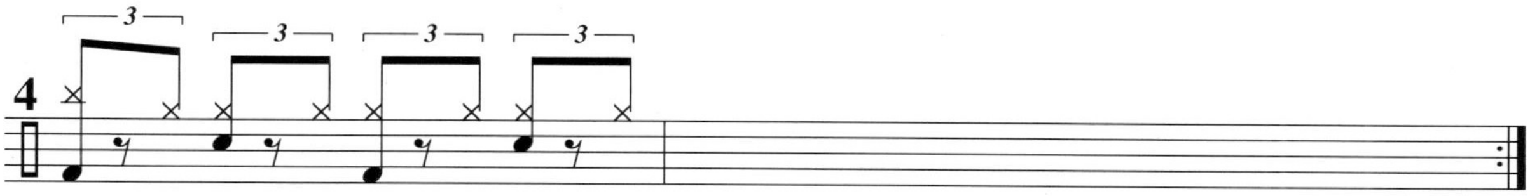
CD 61
1:39

5

CD 61
2:12

6
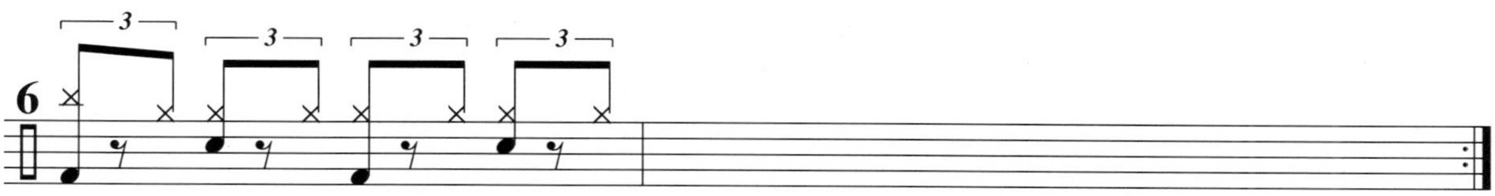
CD 61
2:45

7
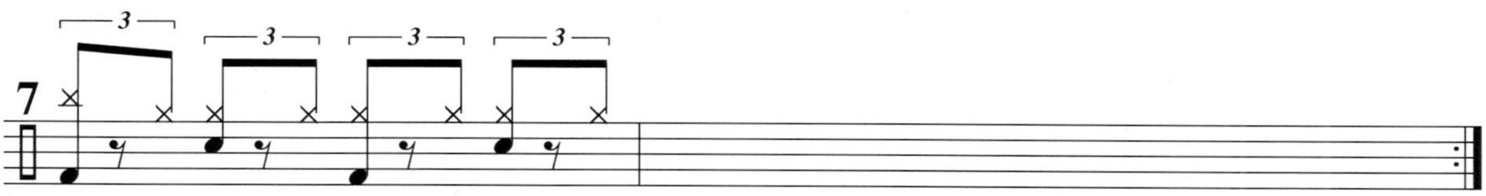
CD 61
3:18

8
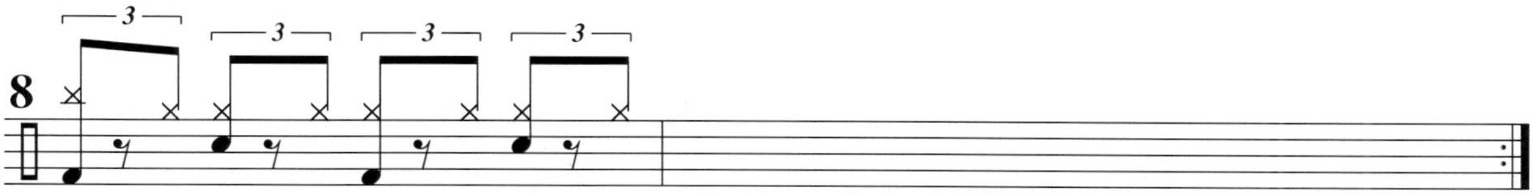
CD 61
3:51

9
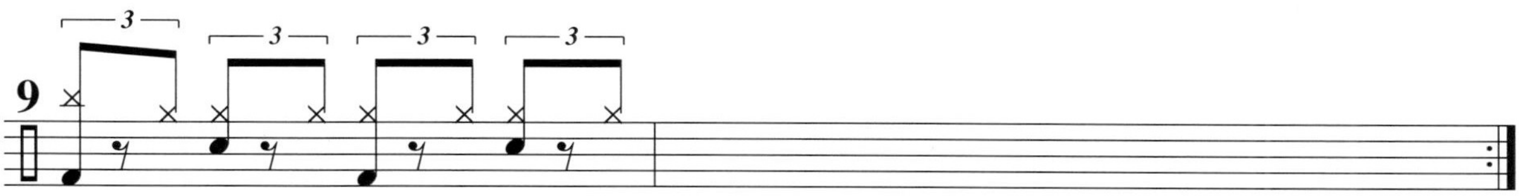
CD 61
4:25

THE ANSWERS ARE ON PAGE 82

Here are the answers from page 9. (Rhythm #1)

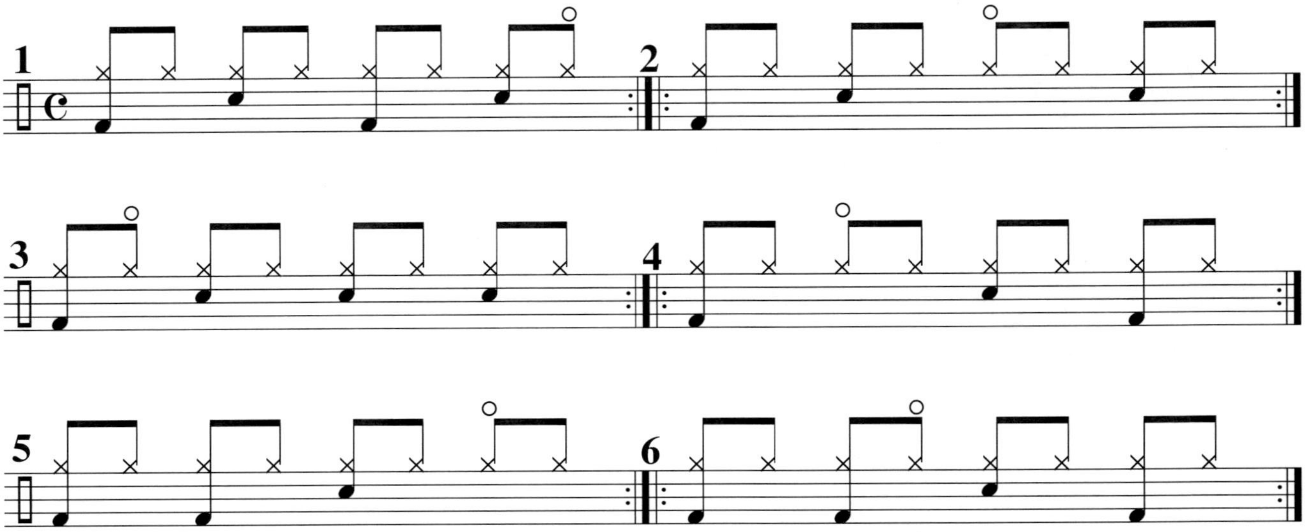

Here are the answers from page 11. (Rhythm #2)

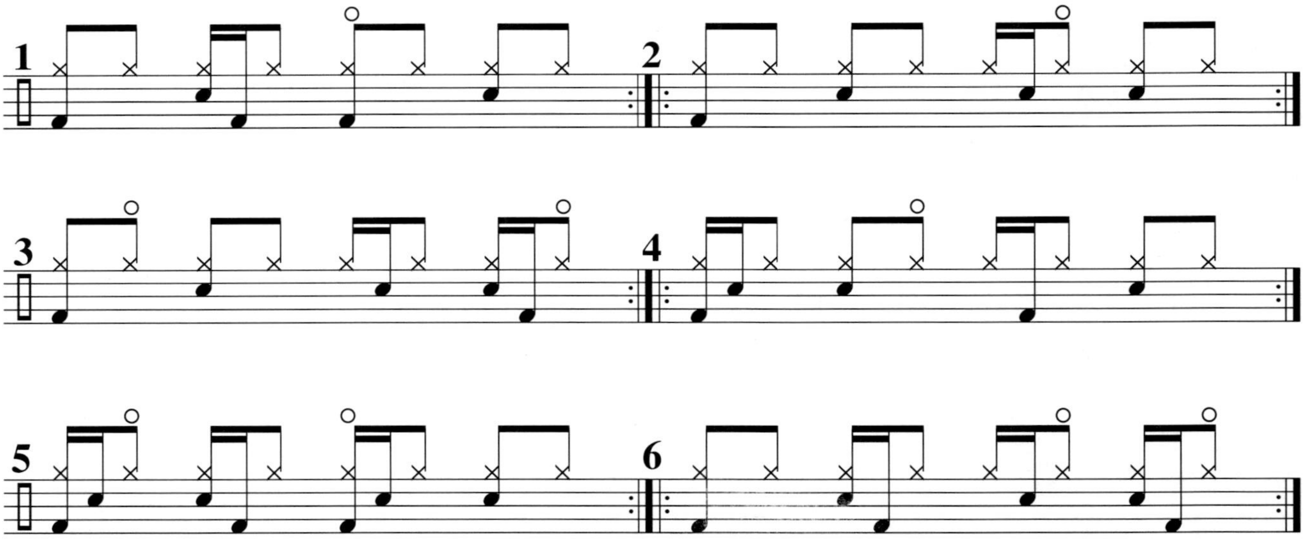

Here are the answers from page 13. (Rhythm #3)

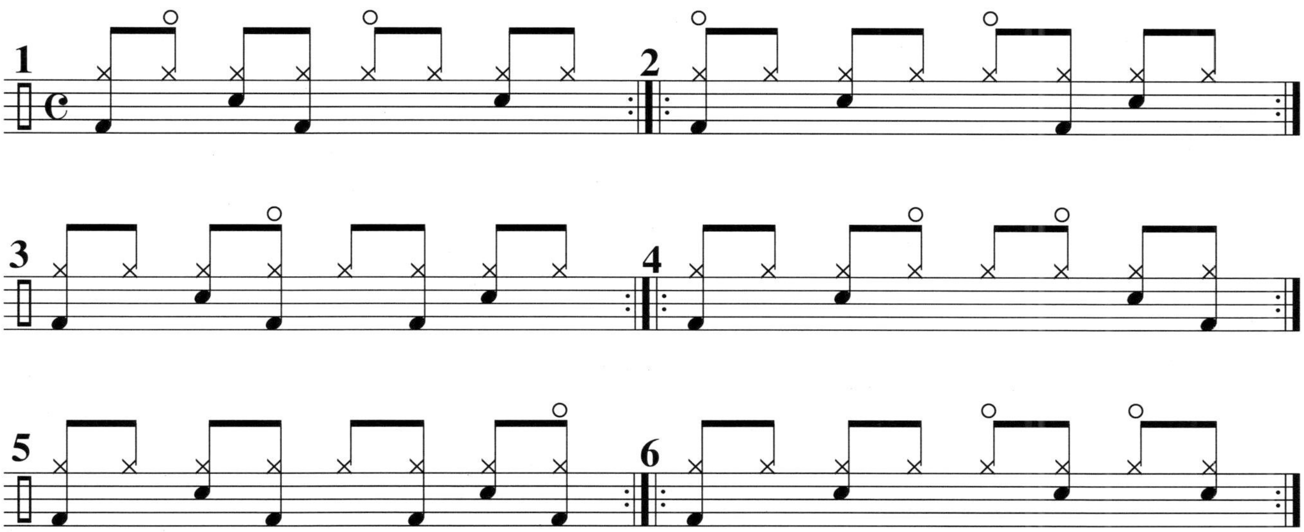

Here are the answers from page 15. (Rhythm #4)

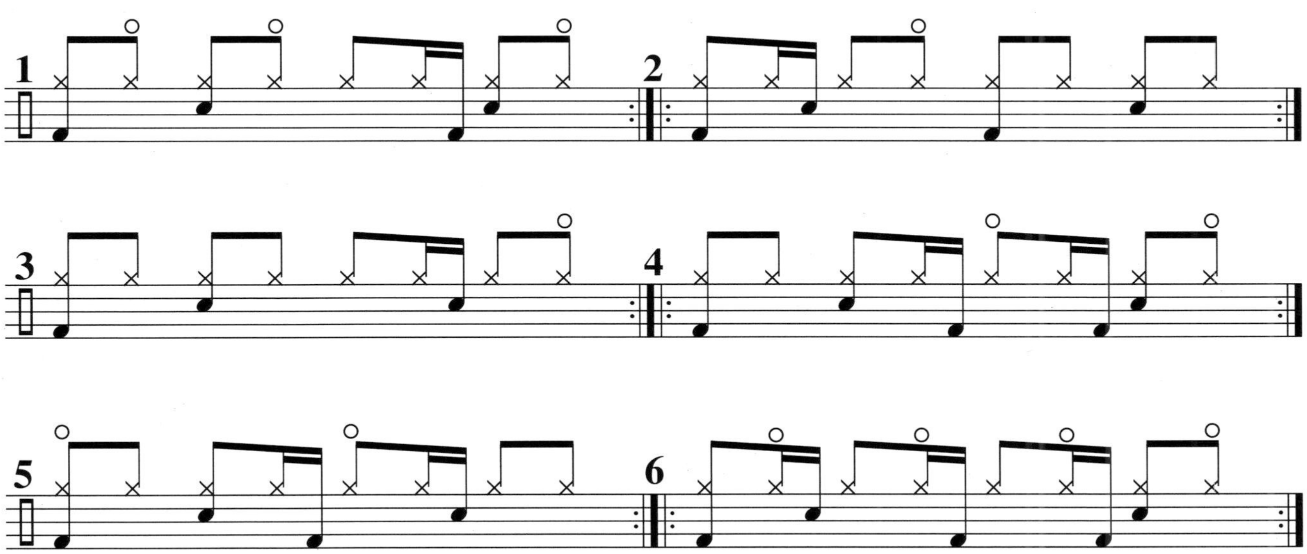

Here are the answers from page 17. (Rhythm #5)

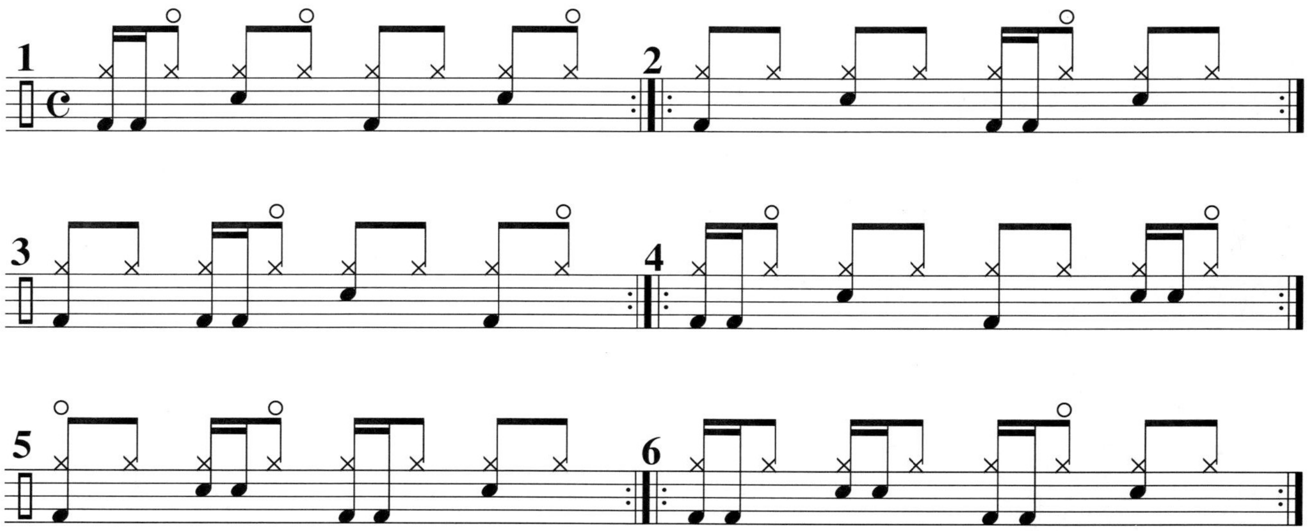

Here are the answers from page 19. (Rhythm #6)

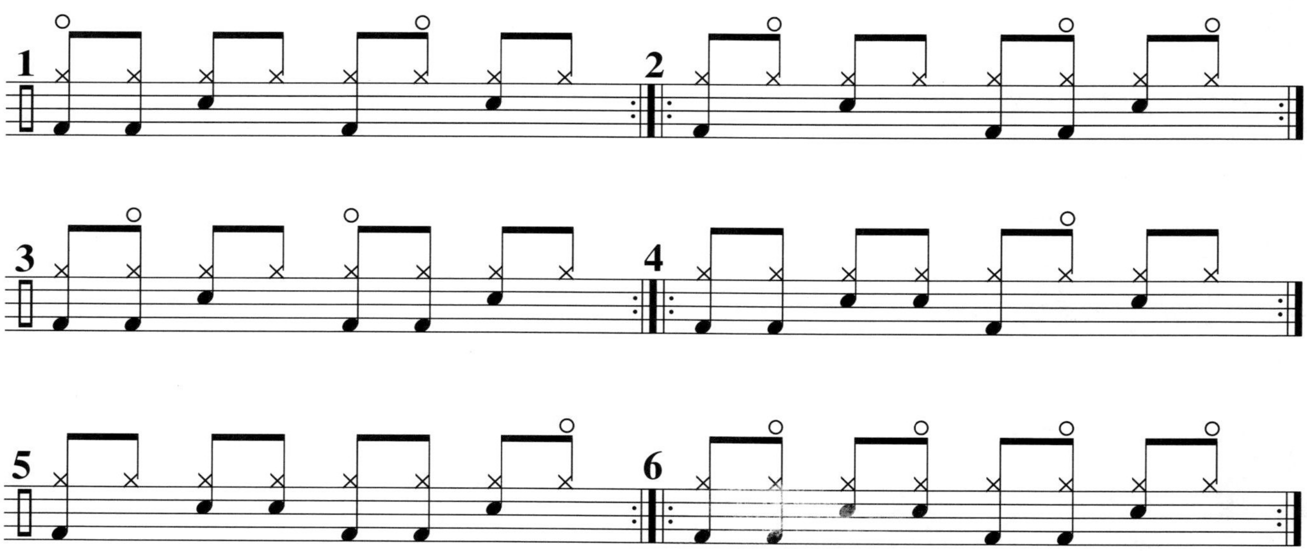

Here are the answers from page 21. (Rhythm #7)

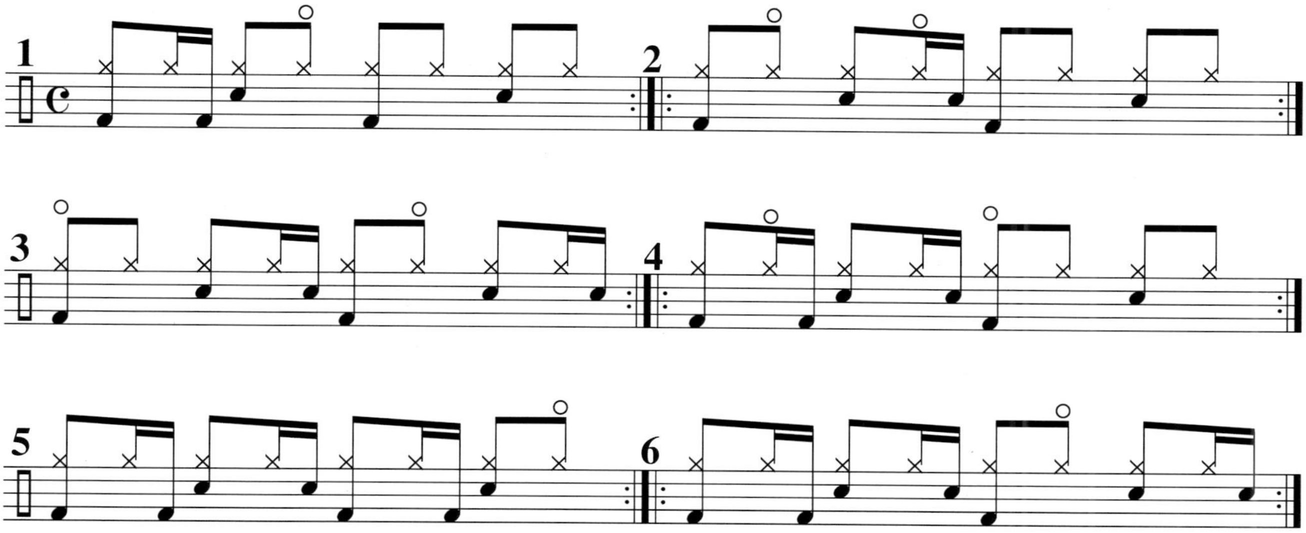

Here are the answers from page 23. (Rhythm #8)

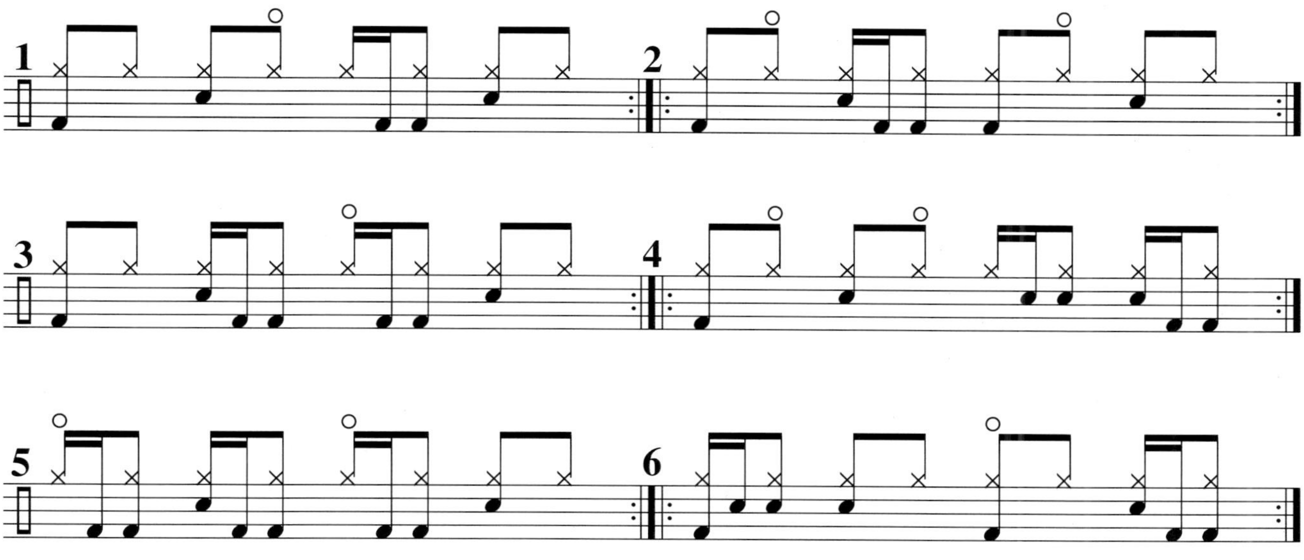

Here are the answers from page 25. (Rhythm #9)

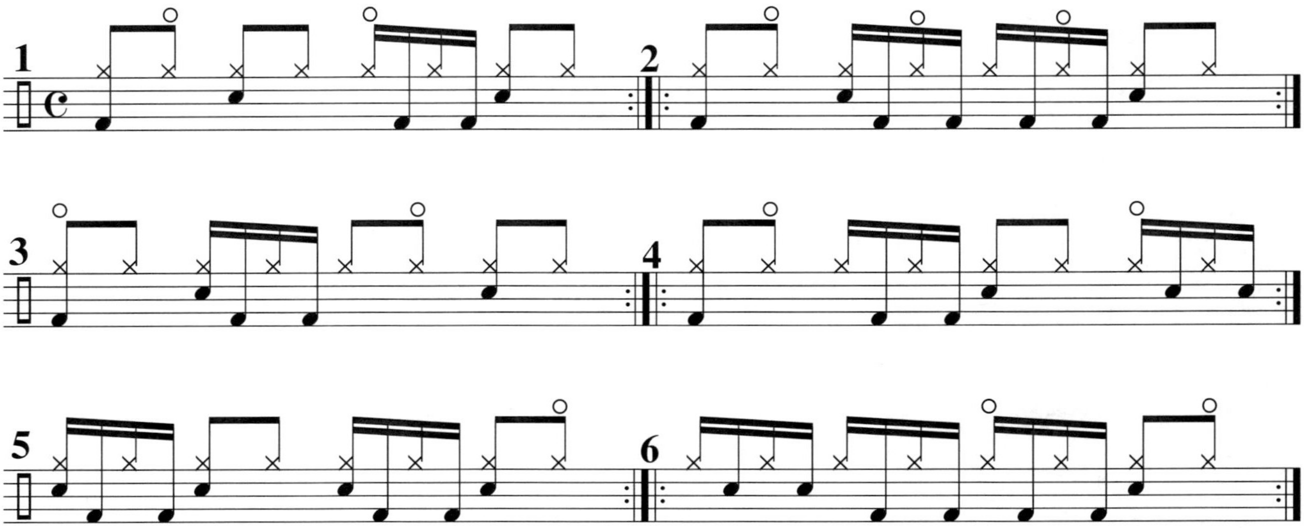

Here are the answers from page 27. (Rhythm #10)

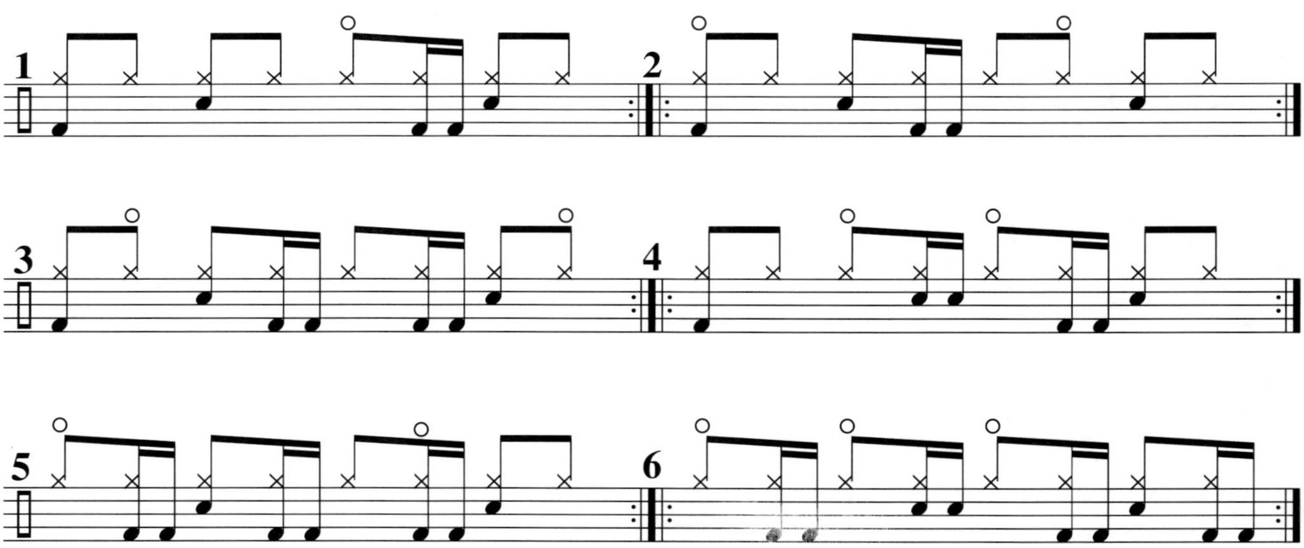

Here are the answers from page 29. (Rhythm #11)

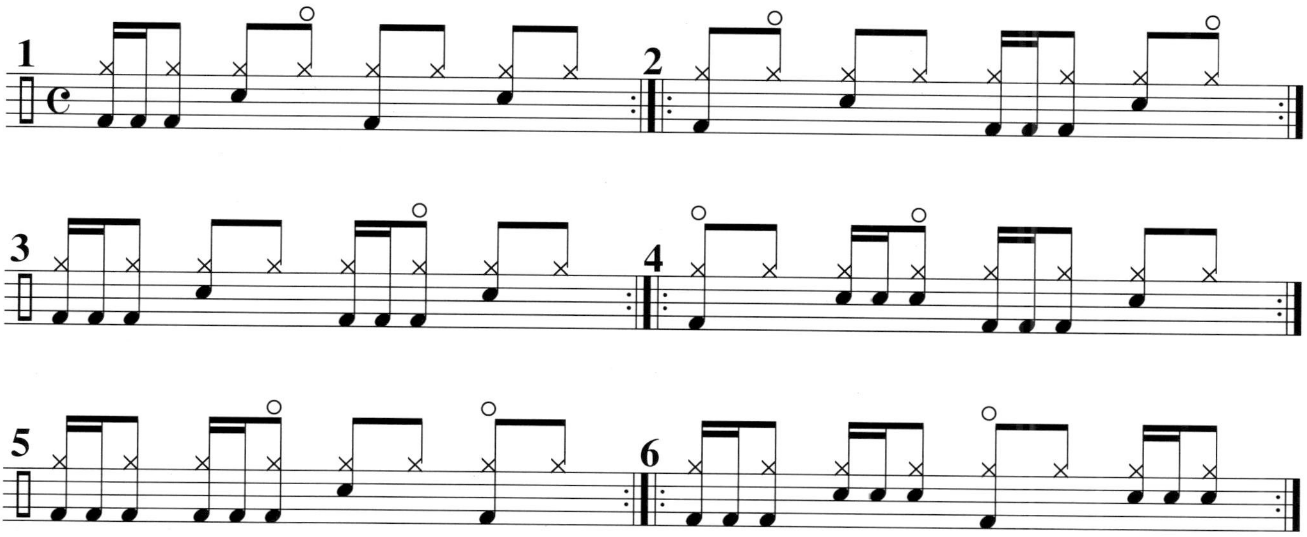

Here are the answers from page 31. (Rhythm #12)

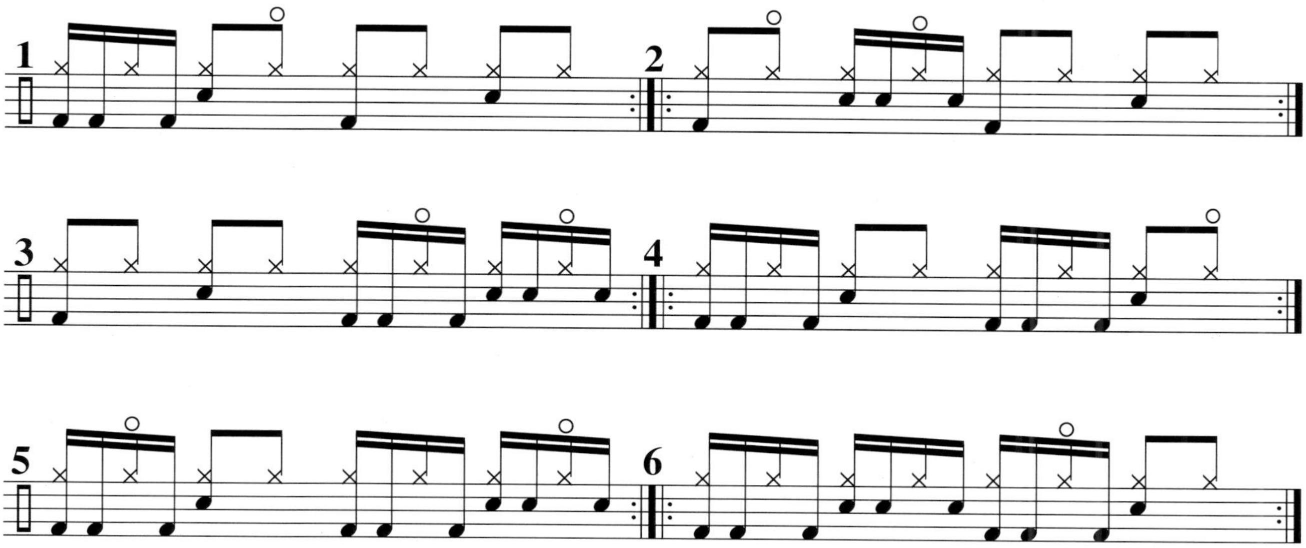

Here are the answers from page 33. (Rhythm #13)

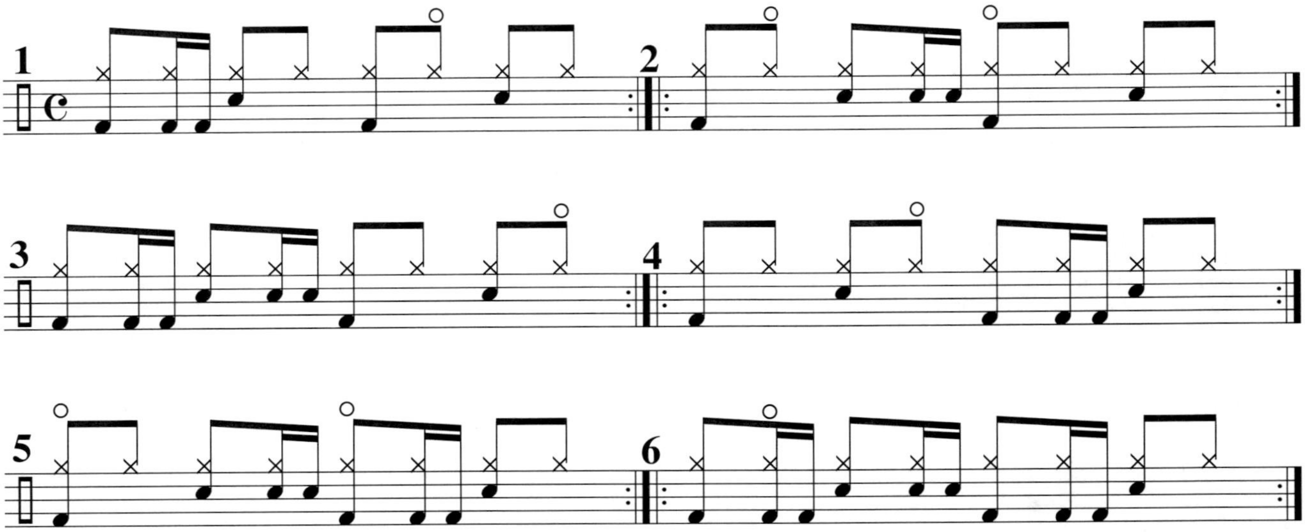

Here are the answers from page 35. (Rhythm #14)

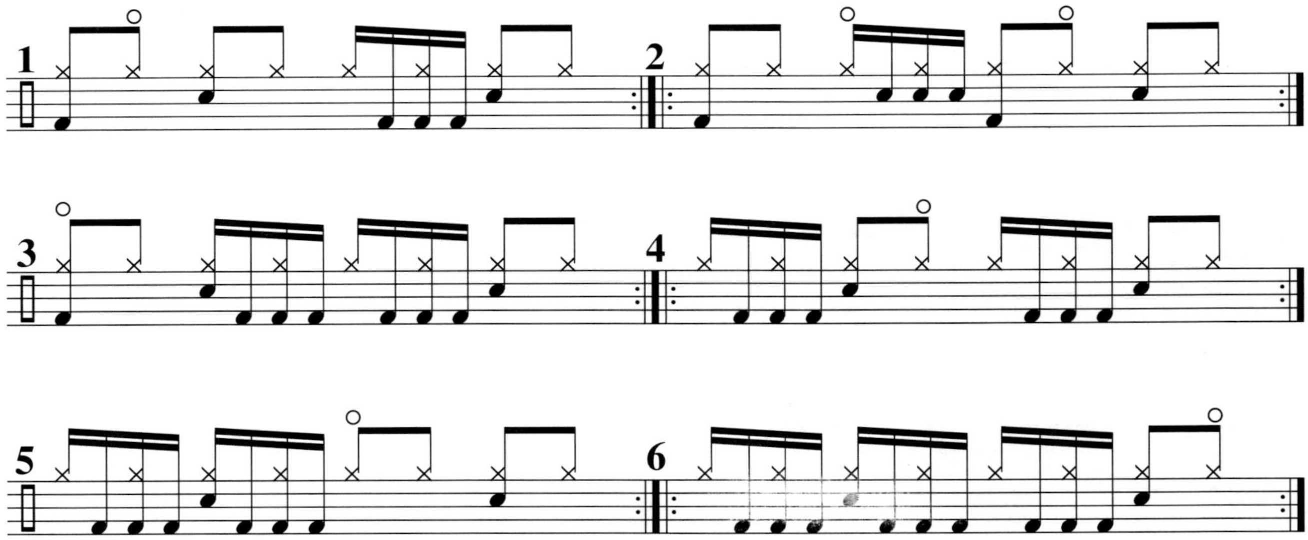

Here are the answers from page 37. (Rhythm #15)

1

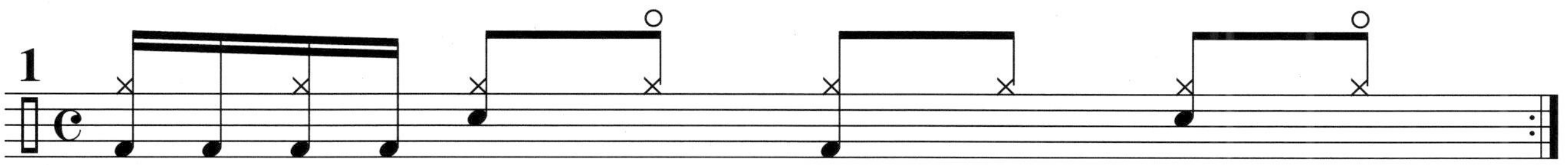

2

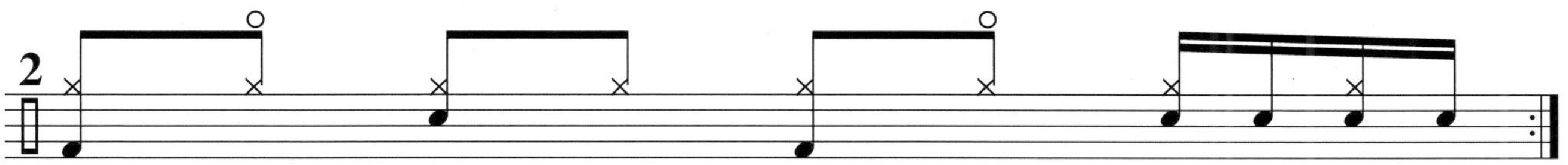

3

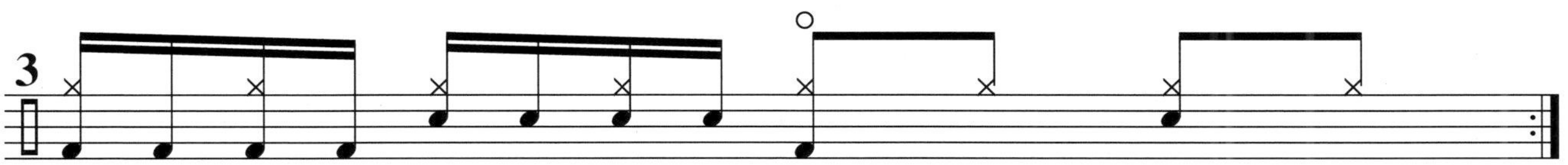

4

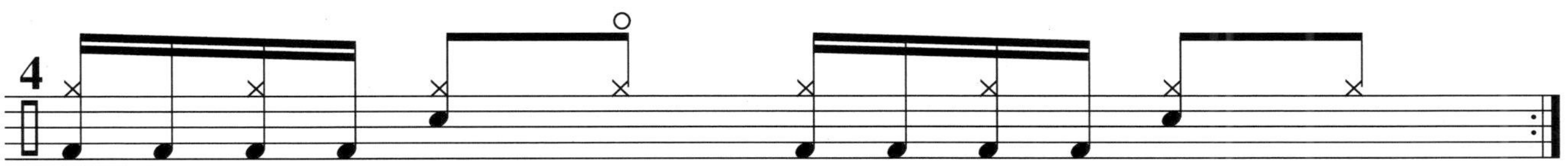

5

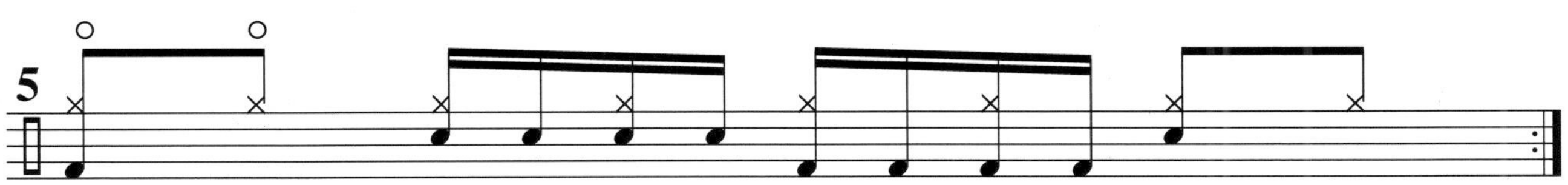

6

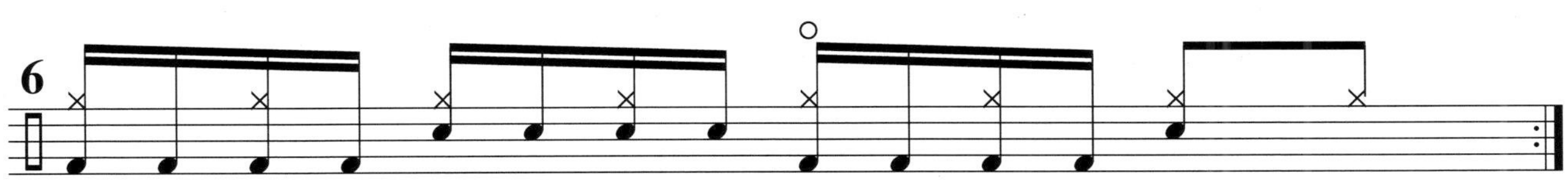

Here are the answers from page 38. (Random 16th note combinations)

Here are the answers from page 39.

Here are the answers from page 40. (Random hi-hat combinations)

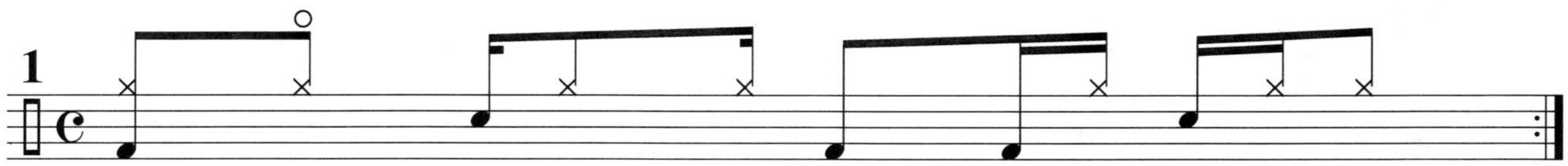

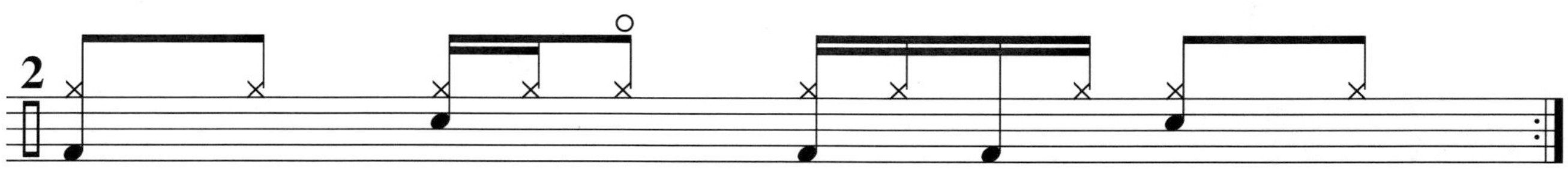

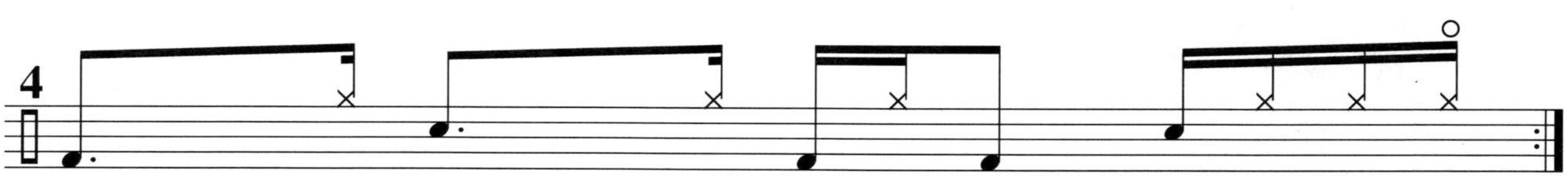

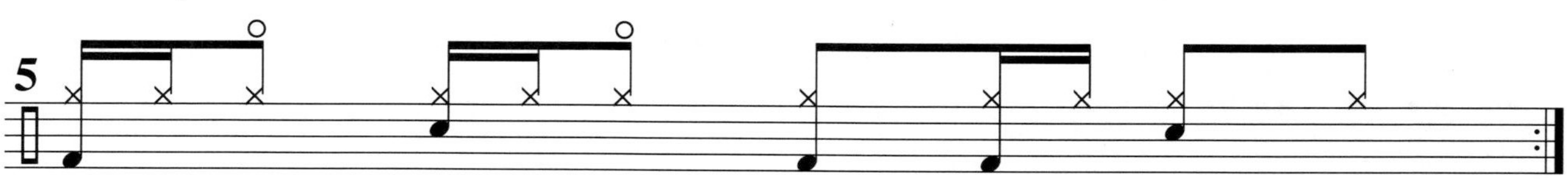

Here are the answers from page 41. (Random combinations-everything)

1
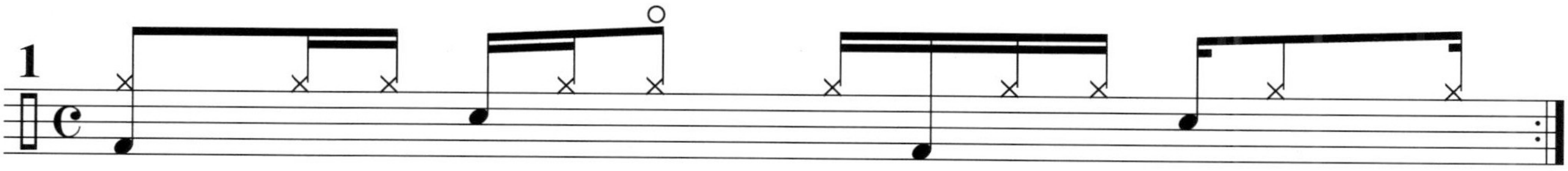

2

3
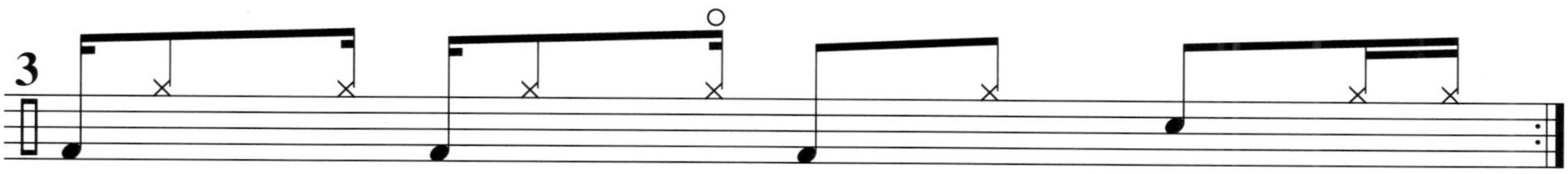

4

5

6

Here are the answers from page 42. (Random fills)

Here are the answers from page 45. (Rhythm #1)

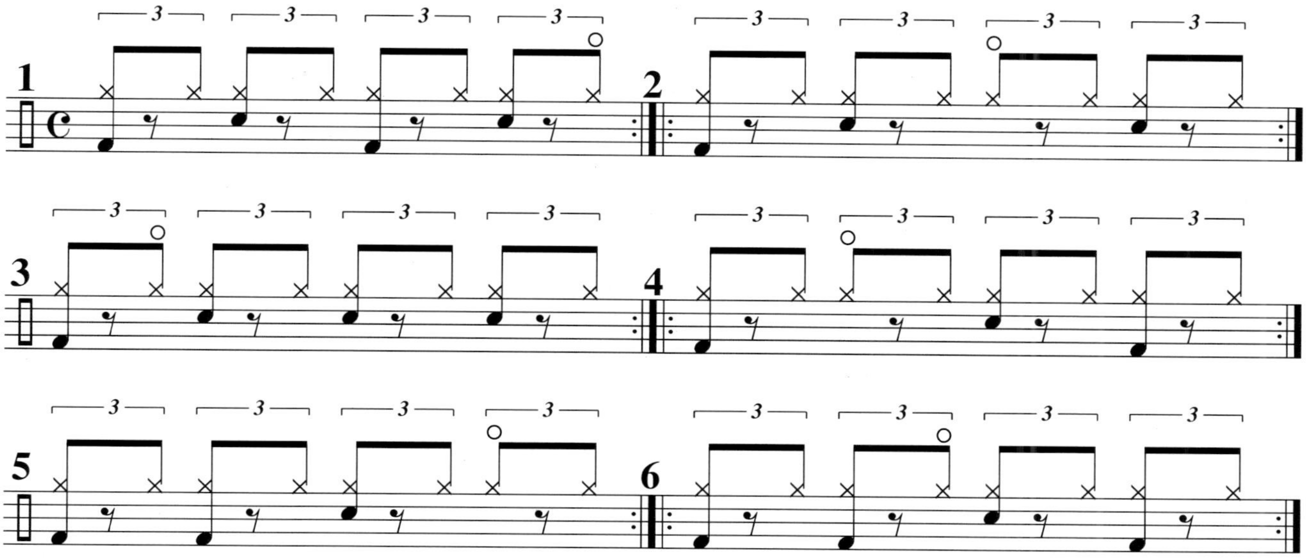

Here are the answers from page 47. (Rhythm #2)

Here are the answers from page 49. (Rhythm #3)

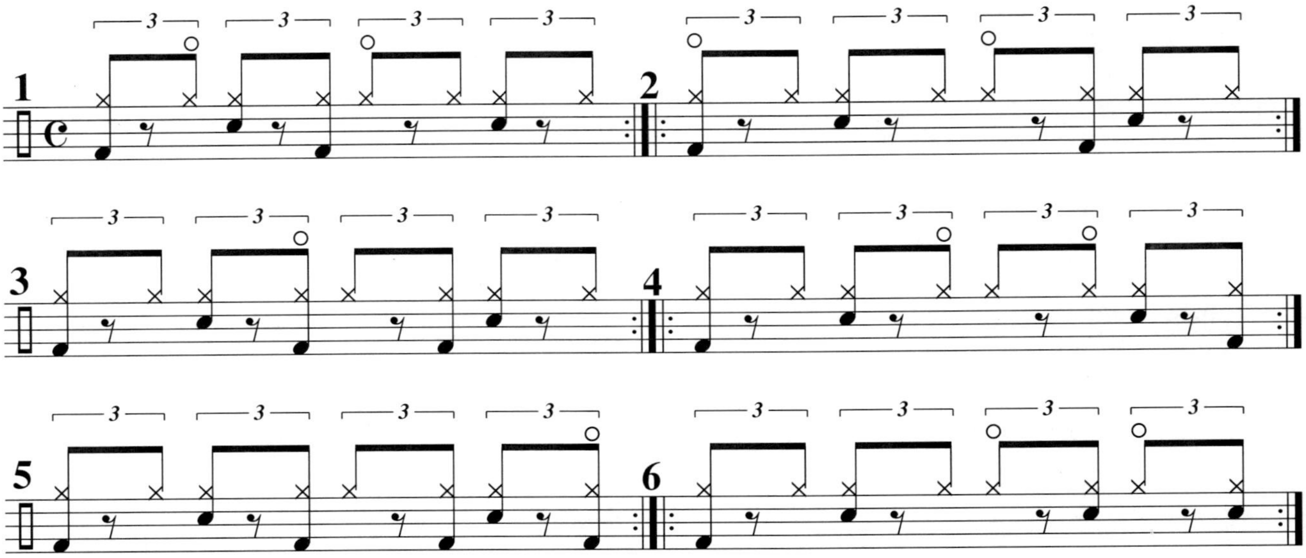

Here are the answers from page 51. (Rhythm #4)

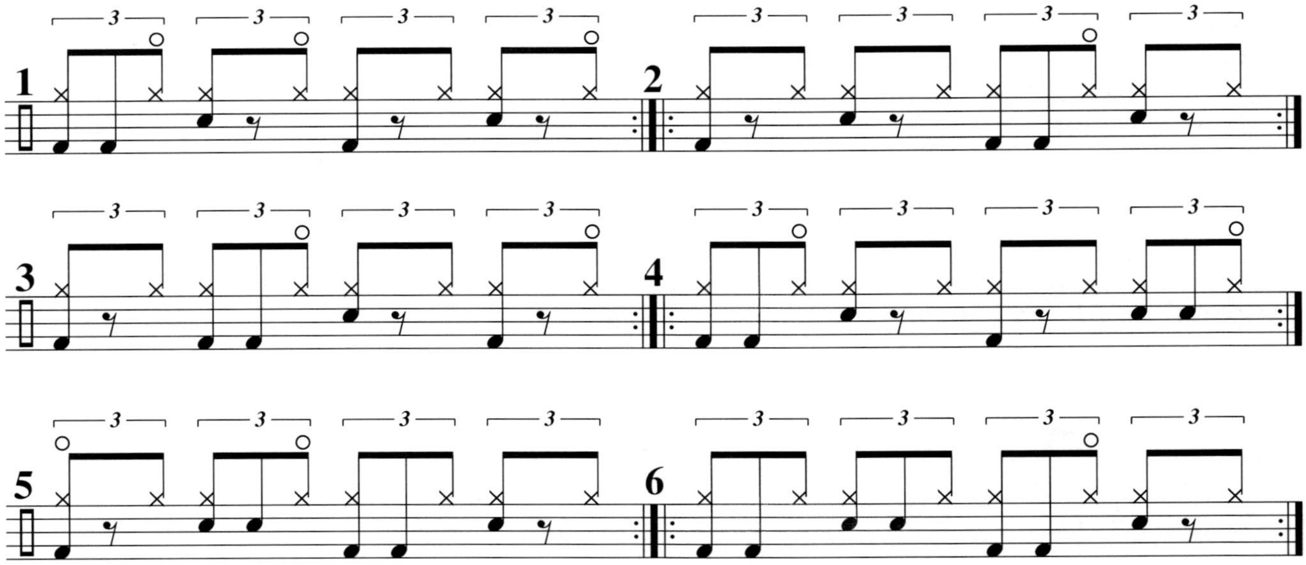

Here are the answers from page 53. (Rhythm #5)

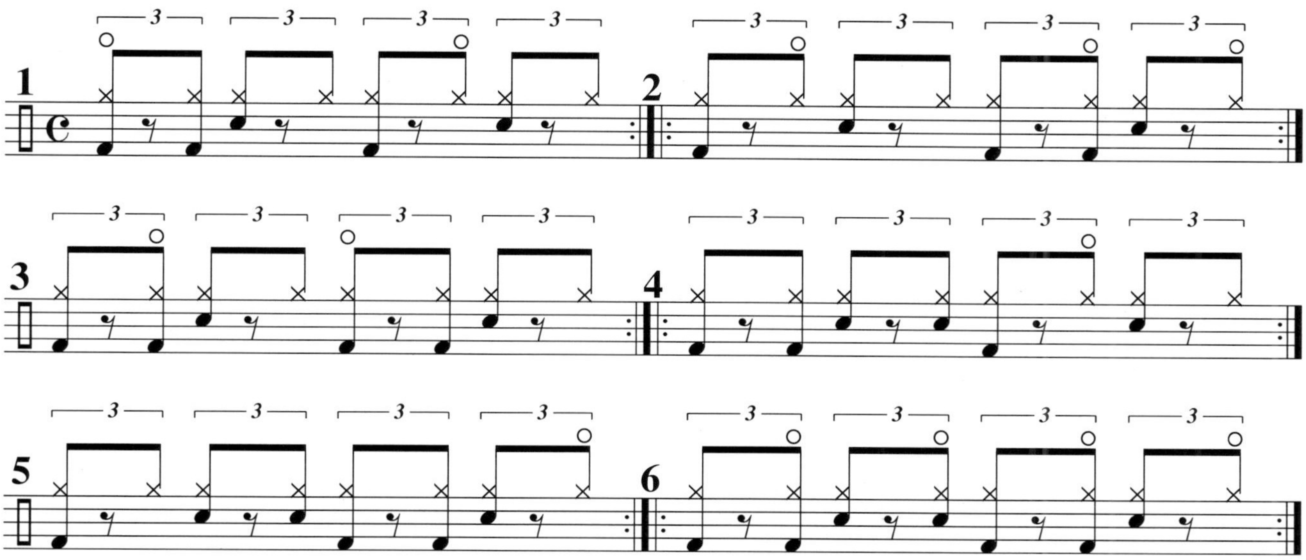

Here are the answers from page 55. (Rhythm #6)

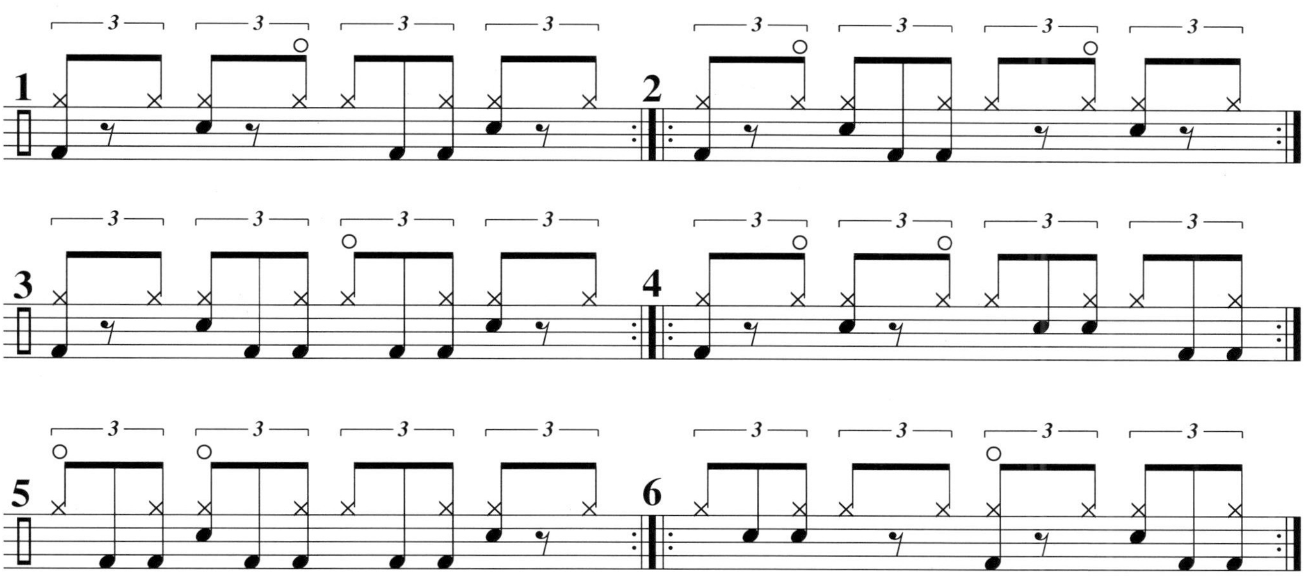

Here are the answers from page 57. (Rhythm #7)

1

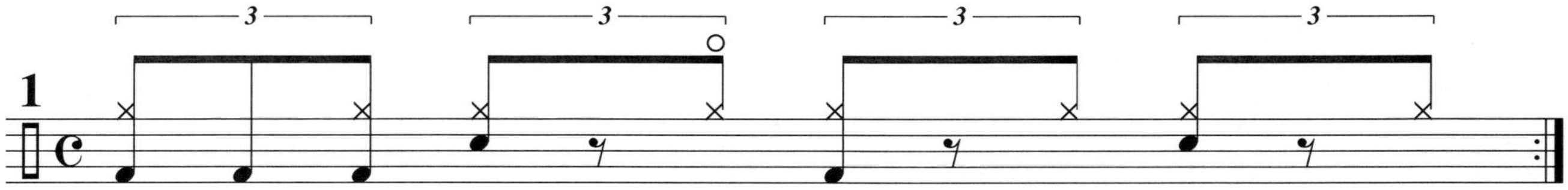

2

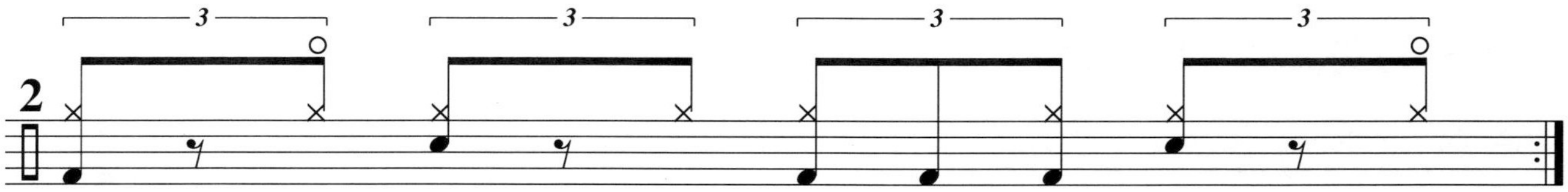

3

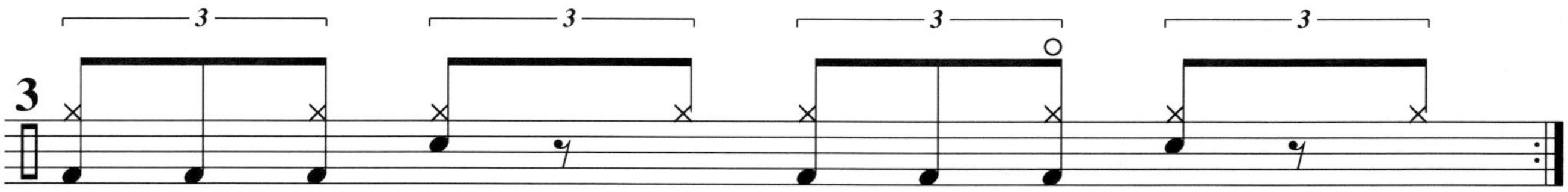

4

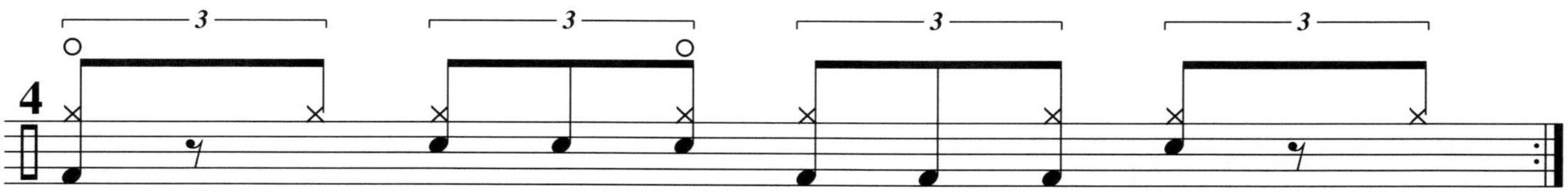

5

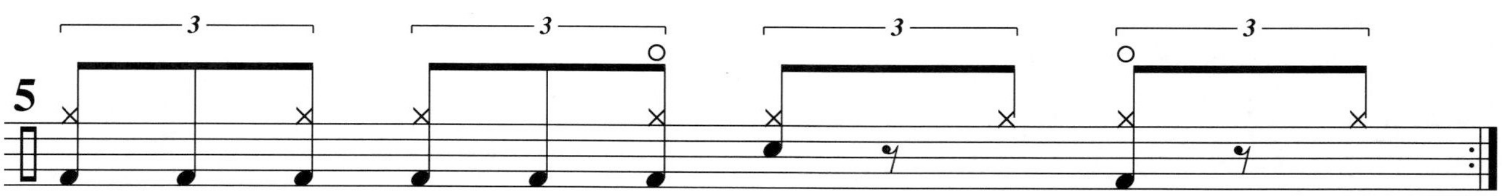

6

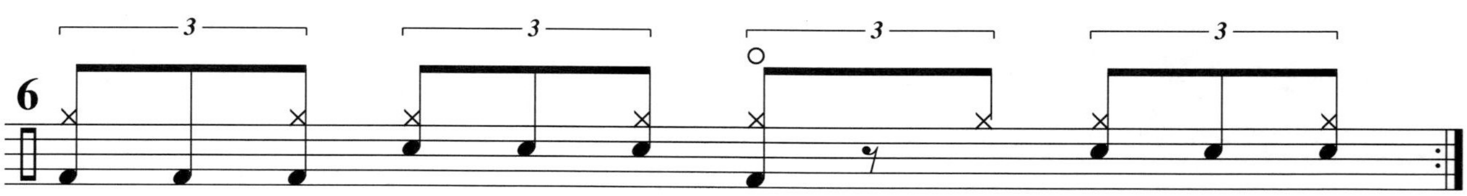

Here are the answers from page 58. (Random Combinations)

1

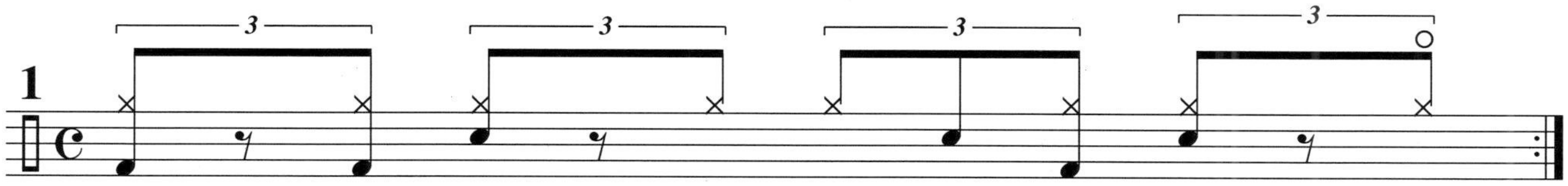

2

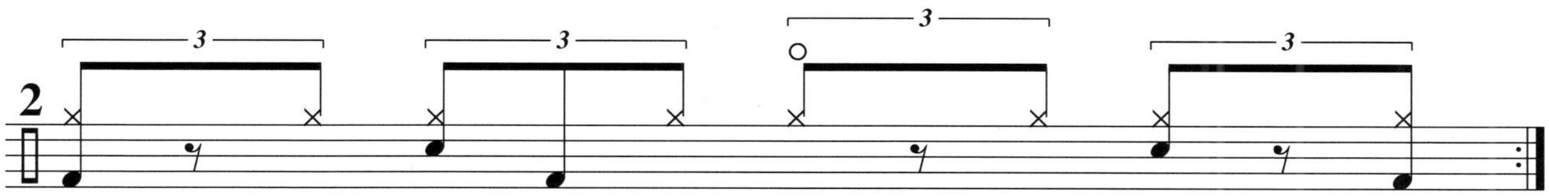

3

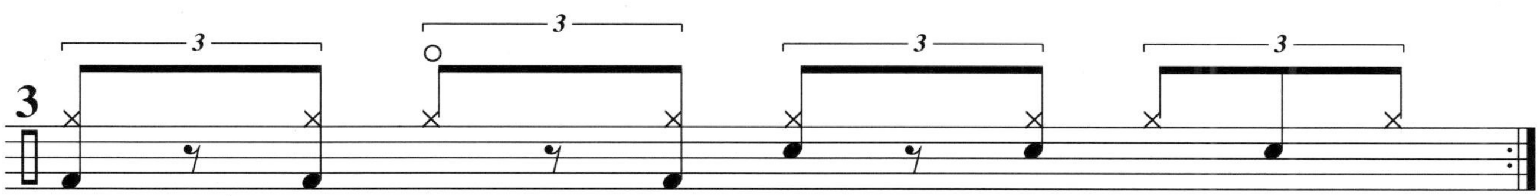

4

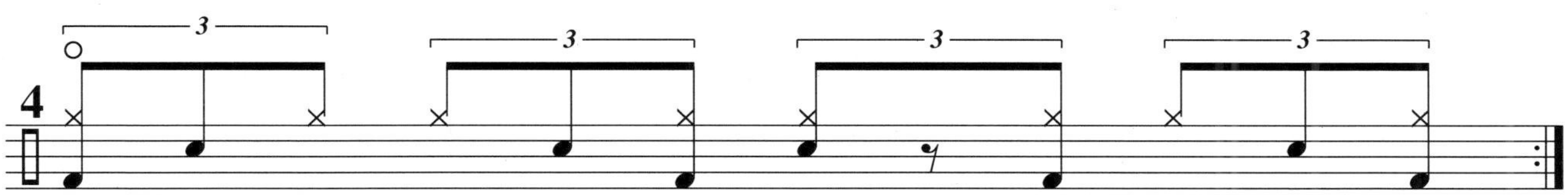

5

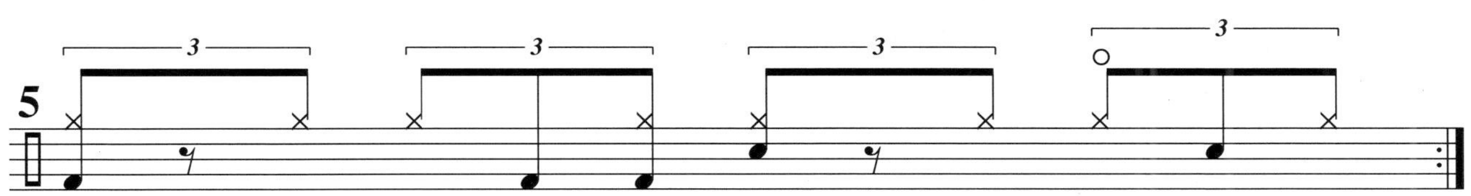

6

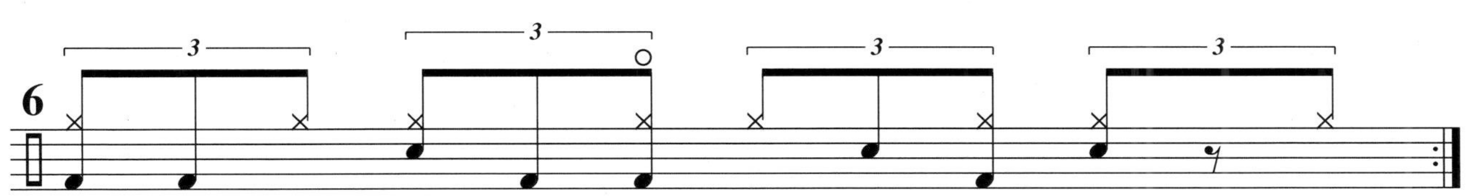

Here are the answers from page 59. (Random hi-hat combinations)

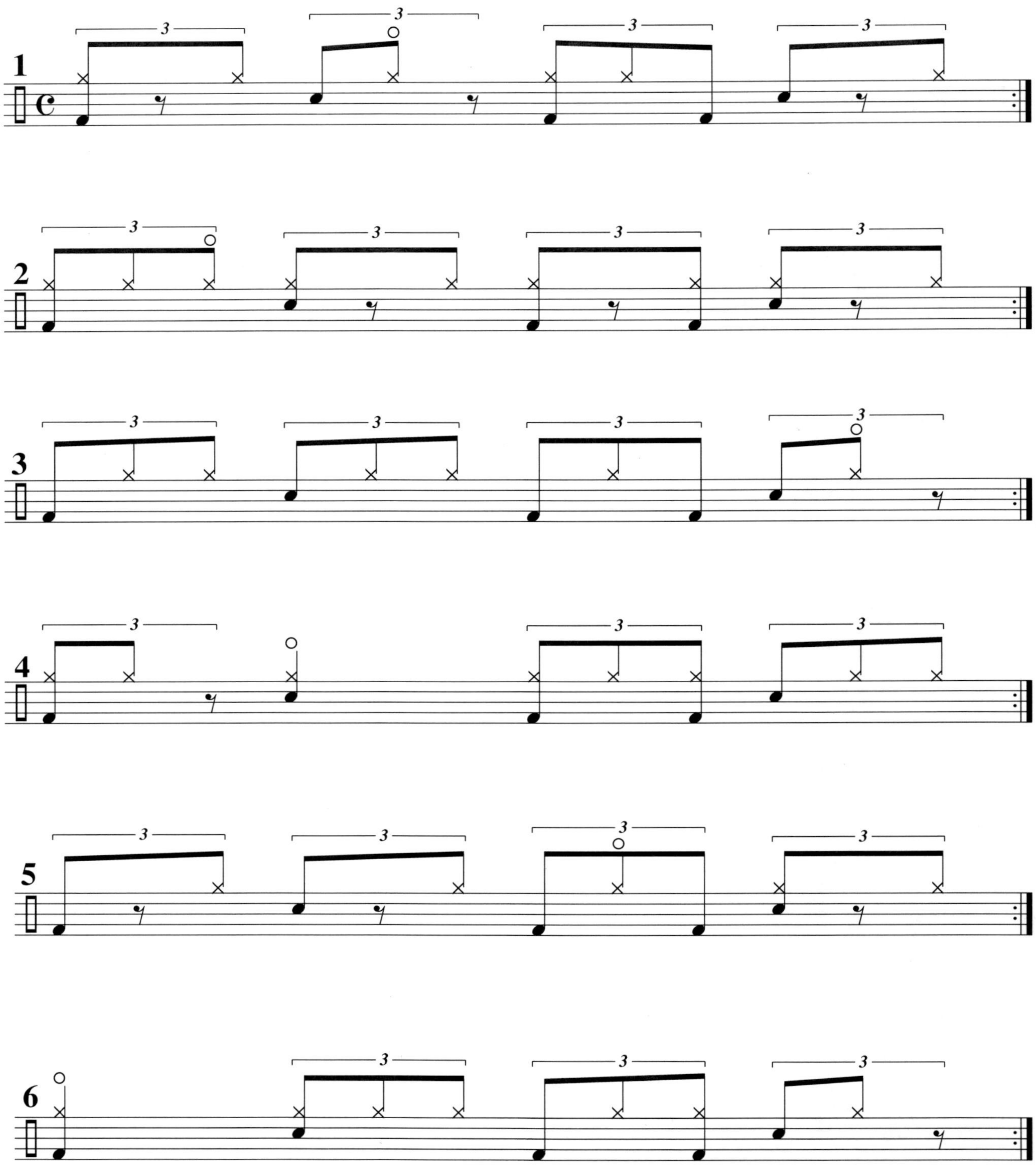

Here are the answers from page 60. (Random combinations-everything)

1
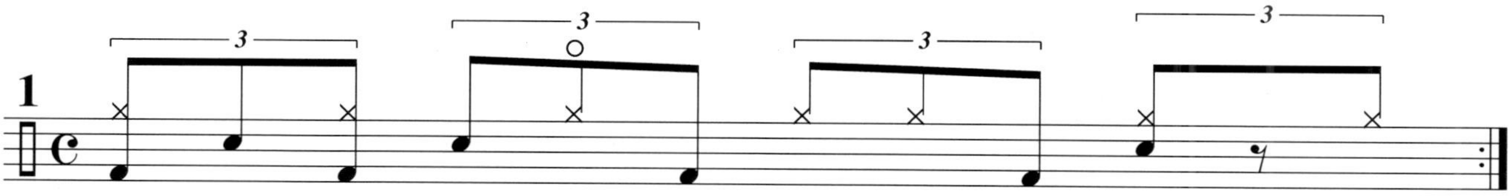

2
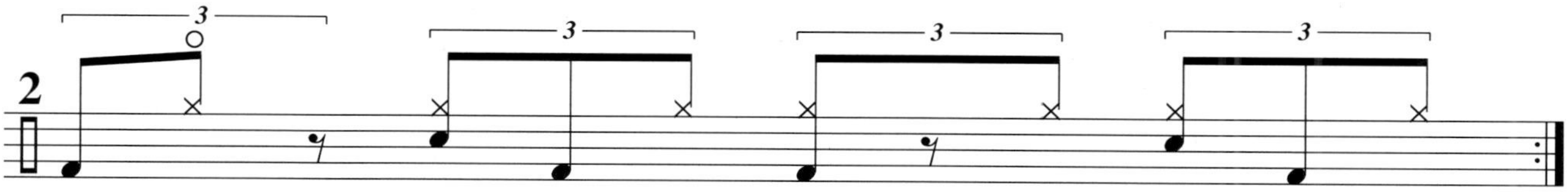

3
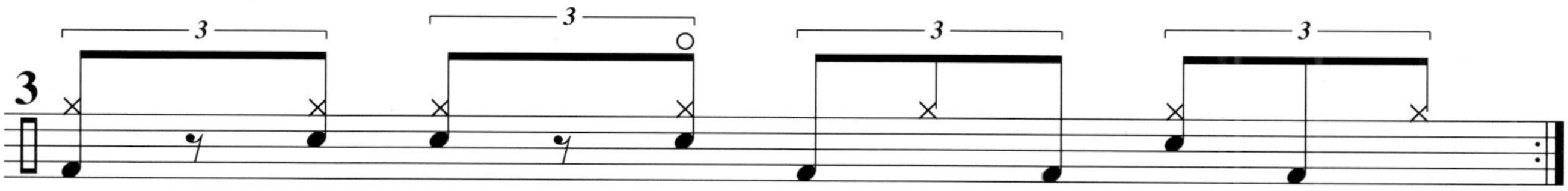

4
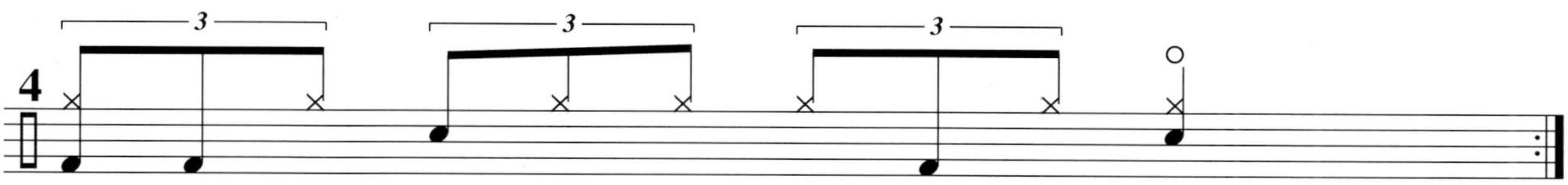

5
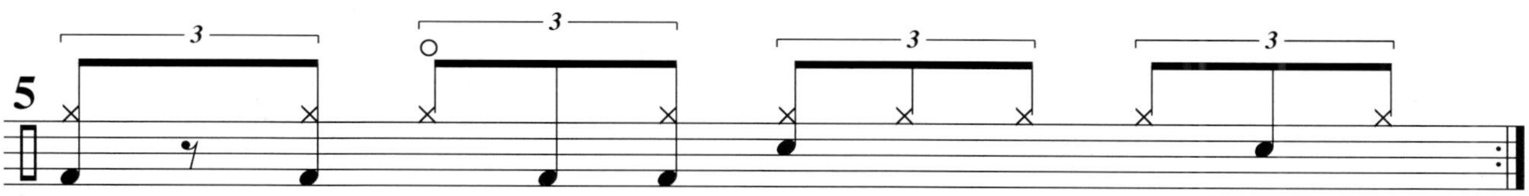

6
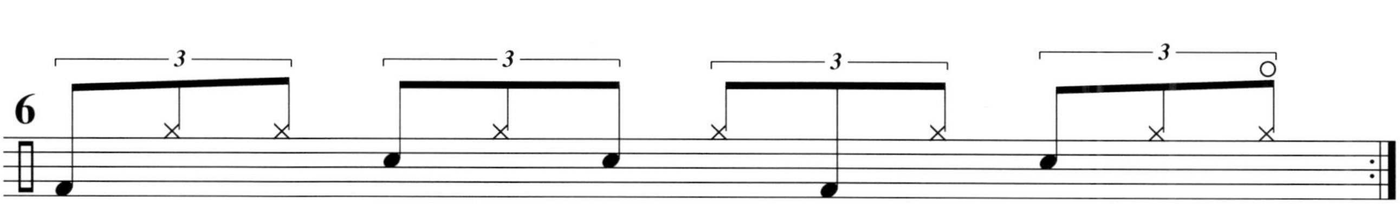

Here are the answers from page 61. (Random fills)

Musical Terms

What are rests?

Every note value that we play has an equivalent rest. Think of this as musical silence. For example, if you see a quarter note rest, stop playing for one **beat** (see def. #2 below).

What are beats?

DEFINITION #1

The 1st definition of the word beat is used to describe a complete drum set pattern. For example, this entire one measure (see def. below) pattern is a basic rock 'beat'.

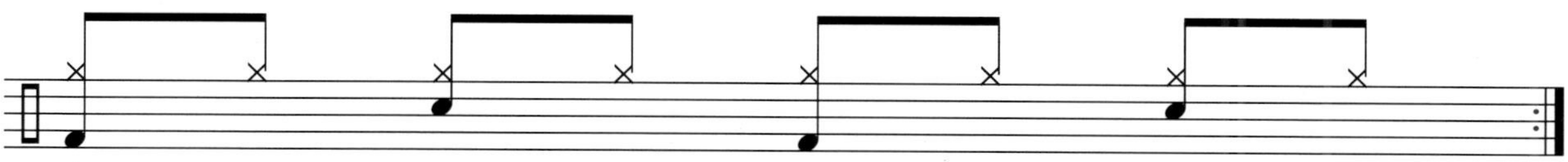

DEFINITION #2

The 2nd definition of the word beats refers to the pulse of the music. For example, this one measure rock 'beat' has four 'beats' (metronome clicks). Notice that the bass drum is played on 'beats' one and three. Also, the snare drum is played on 'beats' two and four.

What is a measure?

A measure is the space between the barlines where the music is written.The following 'beat' is a two measures pattern.

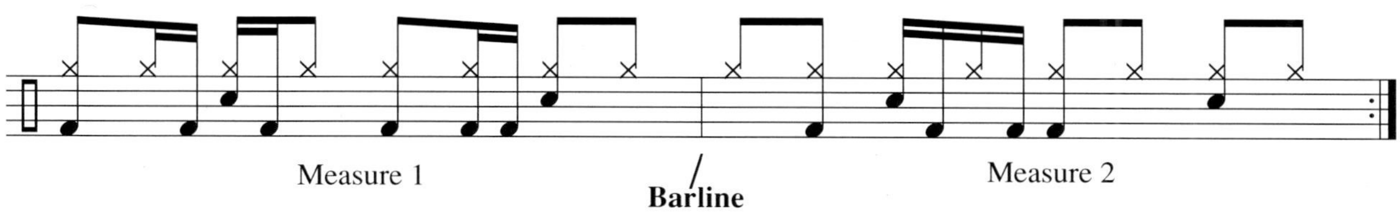

Musical Terms (continued)

What is 4/4?

4/4 is a **time signature** (see def. below).

What is a time signature?

The time signature lets us know how many beats/metronome clicks are in each measure.

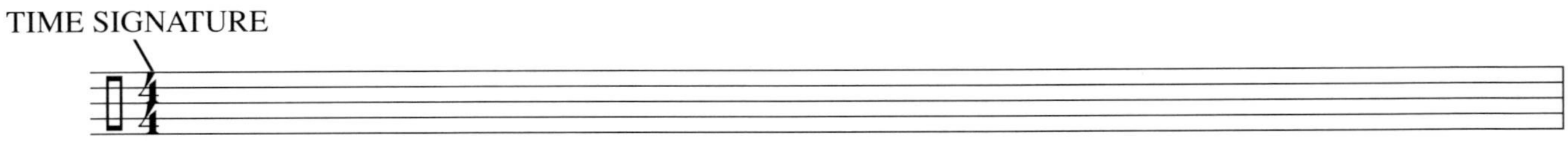

The number (4) on top in this example indicates that there are four beats per measure.

The number (4) on the bottom in this example indicates that quarter notes get one beat.

4/4 is the most common time signature and is often called common time. This can be indicated with the letter C at the beginning of a piece of music instead of writing 4/4.

All of the transcriptions in this book will be written in common time (4/4). The time signature for the prep. exercises will be written in 1/4. This simply means that there is one (quarter note) beat per measure.

What is a subdivision?

When somebody counts off a song, "1-2-3-4" they are setting the tempo (speed) and pulse of the music. As soon as we start playing, we are playing subdivisions of the tempo set. In other words, the notes that are played on and between the pulse are subdivisions.

The following example has an 8th note subdivision.

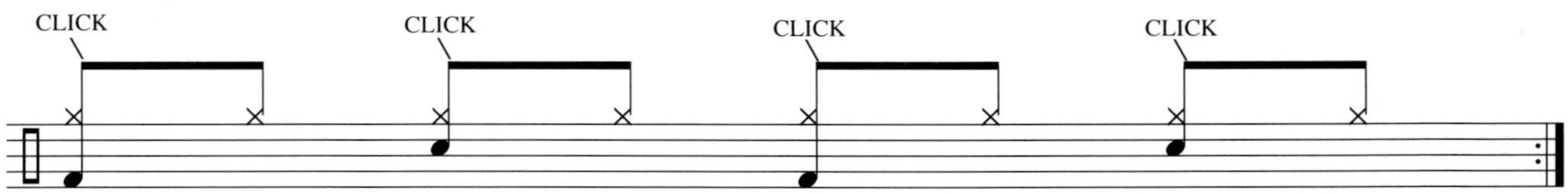

This example has a 16th note subdivision.

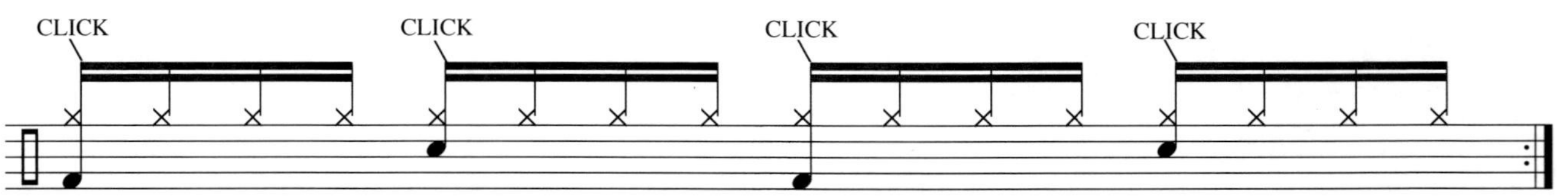

CONGRATULATIONS!!!

You have now completed "The Art of Transcribing-Drum Set Book One"!!!

Now what?
It's time to move to "The Art of Transcribing-Drum Set Book Two".

With the sequel to this book, you will learn to incorporate *more* voices of the drum set, such as:

Ride cymbal
Hi-hat played with the foot
Toms
Crash cymbal
Cowbell
Cross stick
Ghost notes
Double bass

In addition to the Rock, Funk and Shuffle styles that you are now familiar with, you will also learn to transcribe *more* musical styles and time signatures such as:

Jazz
Bossa Nova
Samba
Songo
Mambo
Mozambique
Nanigo
Reggae
Grooves in 3/4, 5/4, 7/4 and 7/8

Finally, you will learn how to read, write (transcribe) and play commonly used variations of 32nd notes and 16th note triplets. You will learn to transcribe and play these rhythms as grooves and fills.

About the Author

Alan Schechner has been playing the drums since the age of eleven. He formally studied music from junior high through college where he earned an A. A. degree in music. In addition, he took sixteen years of private lessons in technique, reading, soloing, and multiple musical styles from teaching legend Chuck Brown. This prepared him for live and studio work in numerous pop, rock, jazz, world, top-40, and R&B bands (including several years with 'Mr. Big' lead vocalist Eric Martin). In addition, he has played drums in almost every musical theater production from *Annie* to *West Side Story.* Alan also won first place in the northwest region of the United States Guitar Center Drum-Off competition and had the honor of performing at the national finals at The House of Blues opening up for Terry Bozzio, Dennis Chambers and Simon Phillips. Alan is a dedicated educator (his students include Steve Vai's drumming sensation, Jeremy Colson) and teaches privately at The Magic Flute and A Drummer's Tradition in San Rafael, California and is the author of the following book and DVD:

The Art of Transcribing-Drum Set Book 1, available at **www.melbay.com**

Coordination & Groove (DVD) available at **www.musicstarproductions.com**

Visit Alan at **www.alanschechner.com.**

EXCELLENCE IN MUSIC

MEL BAY®

Since 1947